Football's Fabulous Forty Defense

Jack Olcott

Parker Publishing Company, Inc.

West Nyack, N.Y.

Other Books by Jack Olcott

Football Coach's Guide to Successful Pass Defense
Coaching the Quarterback

© 1974 *by*

Parker Publishing Company, Inc.

West Nyack, N.Y.

Library of Congress Cataloging in Publication Data

Olcott, Jack.
  Football's fabulous forty defense.

   1. Football--Defense. I. Title.
GV951.1.O43   796.33'22   74-8847
ISBN 0-13-324095-9

Printed in the United States of America

Why This Book?

The reason for writing this book is to help answer the many questions my fellow coaches have asked me via the phone, letter, at clinics, or just general bull sessions pertaining to our multi-defensive organization. Coaches are constantly concerned with: What is your defensive numbering system? How do you stunt so effectively from a multi-defensive package? What are your blitzing linebackers' assignments and responsibilities? What defensive drills do you use to perfect your defensive ends' techniques? How do you defend the Triple Option? What defensive stunts do you use to take away the cut or sprint draw play?

Upon receiving these requests, I would return an answer by mail or phone and invariably the coaches would request additional information pertaining to specific defensive coaching points to stop a particular offensive maneuver. I found I was spending a great deal of the day corresponding with these coaches; therefore, I decided to put together a booklet covering the most popular questions coaches asked. Questions continued pertaining to this defensive booklet; therefore, I decided to write this book containing the complete drills, diagrams, and teaching points necessary to coach this multi-defensive package. 1826391

The author has attempted to reveal all of the secret coaching techniques and fundamentals necessary to defend the most powerful offensive running and passing attacks in today's football. The basic Forty Defenses were constructed to confuse the opposition's offense with a variation of defensive alignments, stunts, and games. The simplicity of the interior stunting, blitzing perimeter, and continually changing secondary calls often confuse the bigger and stronger offensive players.

The simplicity and flexibility of the basic Forty Defensive package will be of great interest to the most experienced coach as well as the novice coach. The author has attempted to cover each defense and each technique in a detailed step-by-step approach. The reader will find a smooth transition of defensive techniques and assignments from one defense to the following defense.

All of the fundamentals, techniques, and defensive assignments to both the offensive split and tight end's side are discussed and diagrammed in detail. The flexible, yet hard nosed, approach is described clearly so that the reader will be able to adjust or integrate many of the author's ideas into his own personal defensive program.

Jack Olcott

Contents

4   Forty Defense Teaching Philosophy *(Continued)*

Responsibilities ● Middle Linebacker Eliminates Interior Splits with a Call ● Middle Linebacker Drills (Forty Defense) ● Coaching L̇inebacker's Shedding Techniques ● Selecting and Coaching the Strong Outside Linebackers "66" ● Strong Side Linebacker ● Selecting and Coaching the Weak Outside Linebacker ● Weak Side Linebacker (Regular Position) "66" ● Outside Linebacker Drills (Forty Defense) ● Evaluating Teaching After Practice Drills ● Check List for Evaluation of Linebackers in Drills ● Coaching Progression Explosion From a Four Point Stance ● Coaching Defensive Down Linemen Techniques ● Coaching the Defensive Loop Technique

5   Split Forty Defense   88

Tackles–"23" ● Inside Linebackers–"11" ● Ends "8" (or "6" to the Split End Side) ● Outside Linebacker–"65" or "66" ● Adjustments for End and Outside Linebackers

6   Split Forty Adjustments and Stunts   102

Split 40 Defense 1-2-3 Blitzes ● Split Forty Middle Stunts ● Additional Split Forty Adjustments ● Split Forty Strategic Adjustments and Stunts

7   How to Teach the Split Forty Defense   131

Teaching Split Forty Defensive Consistency ● Teaching Pride ● Teaching Success ● In Season Teaching Techniques ● Coaching the Defensive Tackles "23" ● Defensive Tackle "23" Reactions ● Defensive Tackle Adjustments and Techniques (Split 40 Defense) ● Defensive Tackle's Strong Side Alignment ● Defensive Tackle Drills (Split Forty Defense) ● Coaching the Defensive Inside Linebacker "11" ● Teaching the Inside Split 40 Linebacker "11" ● Linebacker's Techniques ● Linebacker's Football Knowledge ● Stance and Course of Split Linebackers ● Defensive Inside Linebacker Drills (Split Forty Defense) ● Coaching the Defensive Ends "6" and "8" ● The Split Forty Wide Defense ● Defensive End ("8") Technique ● Defensive End's Drills (Split Forty Defense) ● Tackle with the Shoulders Parallel to the Goal Line ● Tackling (Head On) ● How to Coaching Tackling ● Defensive Tackling Drills ● Coaching the Outside Linebackers "65"–"66" ● Split, Weak, or Short Side Adjustments ● Double Cover ("9" Technique) ● Pass Coverage Responsibility for Weak Linebacker ● Spread Coverage Adjustment (Split 40 Defense) ● Outside Linebacker Drills (Split Forty Defense)

8   Coaching Forty Over and Under Defense   187

Forty Over and Under Calls ● Defensive End and Linebacker Play "67" ● Defensive Tackle and End Play "45" ● Defensive Linebacker Play "332" ● Defensive Nose Tackle Play "0" ● Defensive Cornerback Play ● Defensive Safetyman Play

Chapter 1

Defensive Philosophy

The Forty Defense attacks the offense. While many defensive teams are content to slow down or delay their opponent's offense, our philosophy is to go after and attack the offensive play before the offense has a chance to get started. This does not mean we are consistently blitzing linebackers, but it means our defensive linemen and linebackers are coached to be aggressive and go after the ball carrier rather than catch the offensive blocker and then contain the ball carrier. Therefore, we teach our defenders to control the line of scrimmage and carry the attack to the offense by forcing and pressurizing the offense into making both physical and mental mistakes. Along with forcing and pressurizing the offense, we emphasize that our defenders must also contain the opposition's wide power sweeps, pitchouts, and quick sweeps.

DEFENSIVE FOOTBALL

Defensive football is of paramount importance in winning football. If a coach must concentrate on a particular phase of the game, the emphasis must then be placed upon the overall defensive desire to stop the opponent. In past years the defensive theory was "a good offense is the best defense." Our defensive philosophy is just the opposite of those past years.

Today's gaming and stunting defenses have caused many offensive coaches problems in planning their strategic attack against a maneuverable defense. These gaming defenses, coordinated with a prominent kicking game, instill confidence in the theory in which the defense may keep the offense off balance and often in the shadows of their own goal posts. This constant defensive pressure often forces the offense to surrender the ball or kick in a precarious position and game situation.

The *esprit de corps* of the defense is often the difference between a good defense and a great one. The entire coaching staff must radiate this confident defensive spirit and transfer it to the players.

We know the opposition cannot win if they cannot score. Therefore, we select only the defensive players who display the desire to play aggressive football by punishing the opposition with our "hard-nose" defense. The player who thrives on our combative and competitive defensive philosophy is the type of a boy we want to inculcate into our paladin-like theory. This individual pride generates into team pride which spreads among the players like static electricity. This team defense, equipped with the intangible qualities of courage, pride, and spirit of "one for all and all for one," is a defense that is tough to crack.

In defensing the opposition, we always plan our defensive strategy to destroy the opponent's most prolific scoring punch. If we can force our opponent into playing us "left-handed" or with a relatively unique series of plays, we feel we have forced him into playing our game. When stacking any defense to compensate for our opposition's power, it may weaken our defense in another area, but again, we try to take away our opponent's finest threat. Employing this philosophy, we feel we can demoralize the enemy by stopping their "bread and butter" attack and causing the opposition to panic, thus producing a succession of offensive mistakes.

In formulating any new defensive plans, we usually come up with a defensive blueprint similar to many of the standard defenses of today and yesterday. Therefore, we arrange our Forty basic defenses with a number of variations off each defense. Our planning is based upon the strategy of presenting as many different defensive alignments as possible to our opponents, while keeping our own gaming and stunting maneuvers as basic as possible.

DEFENSIVE FIELD POSITION

Field position is the most important phase of our defensive football philosophy. As long as we can keep the opposition deep in their own territory, there is little chance that they can mount a successful scoring drive. There are few teams that are able to move the ball twelve or thirteen plays without making a big mistake on the offensive team (fumble, penalty, offsides, or broken assignment). Our attacking style of defense also increases the possibility of forcing one of the above offensive mistakes with our reckless, intelligent viciousness. Therefore, by eliminating the opposition's long gainer, we are going to force our opponents to march the ball seventy or more yards with short yardage plays.

Field position to our defense also means we take away the wide side of the field from the offensive attack. The defense defends the wide side of the field by overshifting, perimeter alignment, and stunting and blitzing. We feel if we can take away the wide side of the field, our opponents will have to beat us to our power by attacking our defense to the short side of the playing field.

SCORE ON DEFENSE

In football there is a faint line between the offense and the defense. As soon as the defense intercepts a pass, recovers a fumble, or blocks a punt, the defense quickly shifts to the offense. We prepare our defense to take advantage of all of the offensive mistakes. We believe that a hard-nosed defense will force the enemy into committing a large number of mistakes. Our staff continually reminds the defense that there are more ways to score on defense than on offense. This may be accomplished by:

1. Recovering a fumble in the end zone for a touchdown.
2. Intercepting a pass and run for a score.
3. Blocking a kick and advancing it for a touchdown.
4. Scoring on a safety.
5. Stealing the ball from the ball carrier and running for a score.
6. Recovering the kickoff in the end zone for a touchdown.

The offense can only score by running, passing, or kicking the ball through the uprights.

OBJECTIVES OF THE FORTY DEFENSE

1. Develop a winning defensive attitude.
2. Develop a flexible defense.
3. Develop defensive discipline.
4. Develop physical and mental toughness.
5. Develop explosive quickness, strength, and aggressiveness.
6. Develop near perfect defensive execution through repetition.
7. Develop leadership.

DEFENSIVE PRINCIPLES

1. Destroy the opponent's best plays.
2. Set up a few basic forty defenses for each game.

3. Always have a second defensive plan.

4. Stop the "home run play."

5. Plan to adjust your defenses to meet the ever-changing offensive formations.

6. Continually practice team pursuit.

7. Defenders should play kinesthetically as well as visually.

8. Defenders should always stay as low as possible, maintaining excellent balance, and keep the shoulders parallel to the line of scrimmage.

9. Defensive planning should be as simple as possible for the defenders, but as confusing as possible for the offensive attack.

10. The truly great defensive football players always exemplify the important qualities of the second and third efforts.

DEFENSIVE FUNDAMENTALS FOR LINEMEN AND LINEBACKERS

1. Move on movement—as your opponent moves, you must move.

2. Come to your point and deliver a blow—as you step to meet your opponent, you should deliver a blow, by using the same shoulder, same foot. Use forearm shiver on scrambling blocker.

3. Fight pressure—make your opponent tell you where the play is going by fighting through your opponent's pressure, then locate the ball.

4. Pursue—after locating the ball, pursue in the prescribed channel, regulating your angle and speed depending upon where you will meet the ball carrier.

5. Gang tackle—just as the words imply . . . we want to have as many tacklers as possible bringing down the ball carrier.

DEFENSIVE FUNDAMENTALS FOR THE BACKS AND LINEBACKERS

1. Key—according to your offensive man.

2. Take a picture of the play; recognize the play before you commit yourself in moving toward a particular direction.

3. Never get knocked off your feet.

4. If a play comes your way, attack the ball carrier.

5. Give ground toward the goal line before you let the play pass you by.
6. Deep backs must first think, "Pass."
7. Take a proper pursuit angle.
8. Go through the receiver when going for the ball.
9. Don't get deeper than the deepest receiver.
10. Be a positive thinker. When the ball is in the air, it is ours!

THREE COACHING POINTS IN TEACHING DEFENSE

1. Hard-Nosed Approach
2. Pride in Quickness
3. Simplified Defensive Attack

1. Hard-Nosed Approach

The defensive coach should be a tough-minded individual who has the ability to transfer a hard-nosed approach to his players. This hard-nosed philosophy must be built upon discipline, pride, desire, and the belief in a player's self, team, and defensive program. The coach must have the ability to surround himself with physically and mentally tough individuals. These players must be developed into an intelligent and vicious unit who will get tough in clutch situations. The defensive coach can be as tough on the players as he wants to be as long as his players believe he is fair.

The hard-nosed approach can be sold to the defensive unit by selecting a "hardest hit of the game" or the "hard-nosed award of the week." The hard hits may be emphasized by a special film clip featuring the hard hits of the week or the season. We also keep an individual Big Defensive Play Chart which is made up of the key defensive efforts which help to turn the tide of the battle. The Defensive Team Objective Chart is also displayed throughout the year on the football bulletin board. As we accomplish our objectives, the defensive coordinator fills in the number in the specific box. (Diagram 1-1)

2. Pride in Quickness

The defensive unit is continually told, "There are only two types of people, the quick and the dead." Our defensive philosophy is, "no matter how tough a hitter you may be, you have to be quick enough to get to the ball carrier before you can tackle him."

Quickness can be developed through various quickness reaction and agility drills. We also time all our players in the forty yard dash several

Defensive Team Objective Chart

Defensive Objectives:	Stated											
Shut Out Opponent												
Hold Opponent to 100 yd. Rush.												
Hold Opponent to 100 yd. Pass.												
No Run 30 yds. or more												
No Passes 30 yds. or more												
Intercept 2 or more Passes												
Tackle Passer 2 or more times												
Force 2 or more fumbles												
Block a Kick												
Score on Defense												
Totals:												

Diagram 1-1

times during the fall and during the spring drills. Many of our other running reaction and agility drills are also timed. These drills include running through a maze of obstacles, timed by a coach with a stopwatch, and each player competing aginst one another for time. The quickest team wins. If a defender can't run, he cannot play. Special off-season fitness sessions are held, underlining speed and quickness drills. The stopwatch is used to make the players more aware of their speed and running techniques.

3. Simplified Defensive Attack

We tell our defenders if they can count to nine, they can play defense. The one through nine stands for our defensive coded numbers which represent the defender's alignment and defensive techniques. Our defensive attacking philosophy is predicated upon a stunting and blitzing attack which the defender must read on the go. While our defensive attack may look complicated to the offensive quarterback, it is in reality a simple defensive program. Our staff agrees that the best definition for simplicity is, "a defense that we know and can teach and that can be executed successfully." Our staff also believes that if the defense is getting beat, we should not add but rather subtract. This means that we must get back to our basic defensive fundamentals.

The defensive coordinator must realize it is not how well he knows the defense, but how well he can teach it to the defenders. The most successful defensive staff is the one that can adjust the defense not only before, but during the ball game.

DEFENDERS' MENTAL APPROACH

In order to play winning defensive football, all of the defensive football players must be aware of the offensive opponent's down and distance statistics before each play. They must also be mentally alert and be able to recall the expected offensive maneuvers on each down, depending upon field position and according to the scouting report. All of our defenders must be mentally ready for the defensive signal caller to verbally erase or check off a new defensive call. We play a team defense; therefore, all defenders are required to go through their prescribed defensive maneuvers so that each player covers his specific area of responsibility. There are no exceptions to our team defenses. The coaching staff accepts no excuses for any player "playing it by ear" or on his own initiative.

Defensive team pride begins in the huddle; therefore, we demand that all of our defenders hustle to the defensive open huddle immediately after the whistle blows. Only the defensive signal caller speaks in the huddle and all defenders are required to focus their eyes directly at the signal caller, paying complete attention to his directions. Once the defensive signal caller breaks the huddle, the defenders are coached to sprint to their defensive positions and be ready to hit as soon as the center places his hands on the ball.

If there is any defensive confusion on the playing field, the defensive captain is coached to call time out and to confer with the defensive coordinator on the sidelines. As soon as the ball changes hands, all of the defenders are taught to run off the field and return to their assigned area on the bench. If any questions exist, the coach will discuss these problems with the individual, group, or team. Our defenders are encouraged to suggest defensive strategies on the sidelines rather than trying to talk with our defensive signal caller on the field.

THE FORCING DEFENSE

An attacking defense features hard-charging linemen who have mastered their stunting and gaming defenses, combined with red dogging and blitzing linebackers who will force the offensive unit into mental and physical mistakes. This type of defense will force the offensive unit to lose possession of the football by intercepting an opponent's pass or recovering a fumble. The attacking defense may hold the opposition for downs or force the offense to punt. Another method by which the defense may gain possession of the football is by blocking and recovering an opponent's punt.

THE FORCING UNIT

The defensive forcing unit is made up of defensive linemen and linebackers on or near the line of scrimmage. The attacking unit is coached to attack the offensive unit by forcing the passer to throw poorly off balance, force the bad punt, force the fumble, or to force the offense to surrender the ball to the defense on downs.

DEFENSIVE FLEXIBILITY

In our attacking defenses, the defender is coached to react to a specific offensive man. The defensive man is taught to move on movement, deliver a blow, fight pressure, pursue, and gang tackle. These reactions are bold and quick, and the defender should explode into the blocker, destroying the blocker with his defensive blow.

The up front defenders are taught three basic alignments: (1) Head up, (2) Shaded, and (3) Gap. Using these three basic alignments, our defenders are able to execute a wide variety of defensive alignments. These defensive alignments make our defenders more flexible to defensive alignment changes we may incorporate into our normal alignments against a specific opponent.

TWIN DEFENSIVE SIGNAL CALLERS

Our middle linebacker is our defensive signal caller and our right safetyman makes our defensive pass coverage calls. In the huddle our middle linebacker calls "40," and then the right safetyman calls "3 Freeze." These two defensive signal callers also serve the right to make an audible call whenever the offensive unit quickly shifts to another set. The middle linebacker may audibilize to another alignment; or, if for example the offense sent a man in motion, our defensive secondary captain may wish to change his call.

INSTRUCTING THE SIGNAL CALLER

The defensive captain is our middle linebacker and our secondary captain is our right safetyman. Both of these captains must be ready to check with the defensive coordinator whenever a time out is called. Both of these defensive captains should be cognizant of the down, distance, position, time, etc. The middle linebacker must be ready to place added emphasis on the all important third down situations. The middle linebacker should avoid idle chatter and be available to talk strategy to teammates during time outs, when he is not talking to the coordinator on the sidelines. The defensive captain should not tolerate talking by a teammate in the huddle. Whenever a teammate gets out of hand, the captain is coached to call time out and escort this individual to the sidelines. Excellent huddle discipline is vital to any successful defensive unit. The defensive captain must know the defenses thoroughly, as well as the defensive game plan. The defensive middle linebacker must be a "take charge" guy. He is responsible for our overall interior defensive alignments and audible calls, if the opponent's offense shifts to a different formation just prior to the snap of the ball.

THE DEFENSIVE TEAM CAPTAIN

The defensive captain should never take time out unless it is absolutely necessary. He should save the time outs until the end of the half or the end of the contest. If a player is injured, he should make sure he signals the trainer and the coach. It is his duty to make sure the injured player has been replaced.

The defensive team captain must have poise and not lose his composure whenever the opposition makes a big play. He must always speak positively about our chances to win in the defensive huddle, on the line of scrimmage, or around the bench area. His defensive manner and personality must continually reflect confidence.

When discussing a penalty, the captain must make sure the official explains all of the options.

DEFENSIVE LEADERSHIP

A defense is only as strong as its senior leadership. The coach must develop leadership both on and off the field. Once practice scrimmages begin, the coach should begin to relinquish his role of the "on the playing field leader" and begin to transfer the battle command to his defensive captain and senior leaders. The coaching staff should not continually criticize seniors in front of the squad if the staff expects these men to lead the defensive unit. These senior leaders should be given the role of leaders in all the off the field and on the field practice sessions by leading calisthenics and by recognizing specific outstanding contributions they make during practice sessions. The seniors should be given the roles of leadership in their locker rooms, dining rooms and during chalk talks. These senior leaders are often given special privileges by granting the seniors the first week off from spring practice.

The coaching staff should continually praise the seniors for their leadership, and this will put the pressure on the seniors to act like leaders. The entire squad will then look up to the seniors for leadership. If the senior boys on defense don't believe in the defensive coaching staff by their senior year, the coaching staff has done a poor job.

THE FORTY DEFENSIVE COMPOSITE

The Forty Defensive Composite was developed by combining the College 43, Pro 43, Notre Dame-Penn State 44, Tennessee Bubble, Forty Over-Under shifted adjustments, Stacked Odd and Oklahoma adjustments. It is an organized, sound, and winning combination that has proven to be a successful winner on both the high school and college levels. The Forty Defensive Composite has continued to develop a great defensive tradition. This tradition was established and has been carried on by my dedicated defensive football players who have exemplified the pride, confidence, and enthusiasm which are the hallmarks of consistent winners.

Chapter 2

Why the Forty Defense?

The offensive football attack is a continually changing process. As soon as the offense comes up with a new series, the defense must adjust and counter with unique alignments and maneuvers to contain the offensive attack.

The modern offensive attack features split reviews, effective passing, power running, and triple option plays. Today's defensive combination, designed to stop this wide open offensive attack, is the forty defense package. This defensive forty combination is the only defensive structure that can consistently stop the triple option, take away the power running attack, and contain the sprint out pass patterns. The exciting forty defenses can be adjusted so they can read, penetrate, or stunt defenders to the proper areas so that the defense can defeat the offense at the point of the attack.

It is not what the coaching staff knows, but what they are able to teach to their players that is most important to develop a sound defense. The individual defender must not only know his own assignment but must first understand the entire defensive picture. Therefore, the reader will find this book has been broken down into individual, group, as well as the overall defensive team assignments.

The author believes this forty defensive package is the most powerful, exciting, and timely defense in the country today.

DEFENSIVE NUMBERING SYSTEM

I have redesigned the old defensive numbering system used by many college coaches today. I have modernized it so that we can put a defender on an inside or outside shoulder of any offensive player all along the line of scrimmage, including a close wing or slot back. Using this unique numbering system, all members of the defensive front are numbered. This simplified numbering system, all members of the defensive front are numbered. This simplified numering system gives each defender his alignment and technique.

The reason I originated this numbering system is to cut down on lengthy alignment explanations in staff meetings as well as on the practice field. This system also minimizes the coaches' technique explanation because, when the coach says, "Play a '23' technique," the defender is given his exact stance and defensive technique to use against all forms of blocking pattterns. He knows that the "23" technique lines him up on the line of scrimmage shading the outside shoulder of the offensive guard. He also knows his key, who he is to read once the ball has been put into play, and the techniques to use against all the various blocking patterns that he will see throughout the season.

We number the offensive formation to help our defensive players to identify their specific alignments and responsibilities. Starting from the center and working out from either side, a head up defensive position will be an even number (Diagram 2-1). All gaps starting from the center out

DEFENSIVE NUMBERING SYSTEM

Diagram 2-1

will be odd numbers (Diagram 2-1). If the defender, on the line of scrimmage, is shading the inside or outside shoulder of an offensive man, we use two numbers for this defender. The first number is the nearest even number and the second number is the nearest gap ("23," "65," etc.); see Diagram 2-2.

Diagram 2-2

If the defender is two or more yards off the line of scrimmage in a linebacker's position, the defender's first number is paired (''00,'' ''66,'' or ''223''). See Diagram 2-3.

Diagram 2-3

Therefore, if we called a Forty Defense, our defenders would line up in this manner and their defensive number or numbers would represent their alignments and defensive techniques (Diagram 2-4).

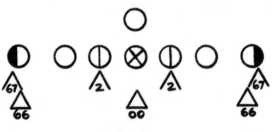

Diagram 2-4

If the defensive signal caller called a Split Forty Defense, our defensive alignment and numbering system would appear as shown in Diagram 2-5.

A Forty Stack Defense (Left Stack) would be aligned ``d numbered as shown in Diagram 2-6.

Refer to Diagram 2-7 for the Forty Defense.

DEFENSIVE TACKLE "2"

Alignment and Position: The defensive tackle should line up head on the offensive guard about two feet from the ball. Additional depth may depend upon several other coaching factors. He should crowd the center on short yardage situations. He may loosen when called in a stunt or on long yardage situations. Scouting reports and opponent's movie breakdowns may affect his alignment and position. Offset, stack, and gap alignments will be assigned by the defensive signal caller (Diagram 2-8).

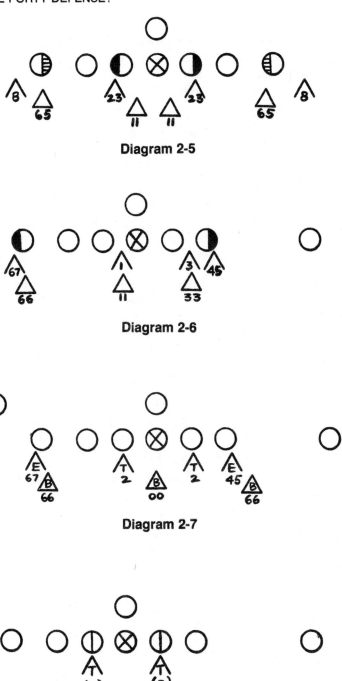

Diagram 2-5

Diagram 2-6

Diagram 2-7

Diagram 2-8

Stance: The defensive tackle uses a four point stance. He should use a parallel stance with a slight heel and toe relationship. The tackle's feet should be the width of his armpits and tucked well up under him. The hands should be about one and one-half feet in front of the up foot. The defender's elbows should be slightly outside of his knees.

Responsibilities: The tackle's key is the offensive guard. If the offensive guard pulls toward the center, the defensive tackle should step down toward the offensive pivot man. If the guard pulls away from the center, the defender should take a set step and then go in the same direction of the pulling guard. If a trap develops, the defensive tackle should insure against the trap with his inside forearm. The defensive tackle is assigned to control the area to both sides of the guard. If a pass develops, he should rush, checking for the draw. If the ball carrier goes away, he should take a proper pursuit angle and cut off the ball carrier.

Variation of Charge: The "2" defender should confuse the offensive guard by varying his defensive charge. At times he should vary his alignment according to the defensive linebacker's call. At times the defensive tackle may be coached to use his forearm shiver aimed at the guard's head or shoulders. The away hand is used to get rid of the potential blocker. On long yardage situations he may use a jam technique, which results in pushing the blocker's head into the ground and keeping the defender's hands on the blocker's head so he cannot tie up the defender's legs. Whenever a stunt is called, he should disregard caution and fire into the assigned area. The "2" defender should get into the running lane as soon as possible and pile up the play.

Pass Rush: The "2" defender should check the draw play as he rushes the passer. If the quarterback goes deeper than seven yards, he must check for the screen pass. Always check the near running back for the draw, as the passer drops back in his area. Rush the passer as quickly as possible and throw up both hands just as the passer gets set to throw the ball. As soon as the pass play develops, the rusher should yell, "Pass!" Just as soon as the passer releases the ball, the defender should yell, "Ball!" This oral signal helps to alert the defender who may be unaware or screened from the passer's view. This call alerts all defenders that the ball is in the air. The defender should tackle the passer from the top down. As soon as the passer releases the ball, all defensive rushers are coached to peel off toward the nearest sideline and set up a blocking wall in the event of an interception by one of our pass defenders.

Punt Rush: The rushing defender must get into the punting lane to block a punt. The defender should aim for a spot two yards in front of the punter and then focus his eyes on the ball. The defender should take a slight side angle charge so that he does not rough the punter if the defender is not able to block the punt. On fourth down punting attempts, the rusher should always pick up the blocked punt and advance the ball. The nearest defender to the man picking up the ball should turn and block the punter. If the opposition punts on third down, the defensive captain should alert all of the defenders to make sure they recover the ball because the ball is in play, and we want to make sure we gain possession on all third down blocked punts.

DEFENSIVE TECHNIQUE FOR THE TACKLE "2"

(Diagram 2-9)—If the guard turns out and attempts to block to the outside, fight pressure and drive through his head. Deliver a forearm blow on the offensive tackle with the same arm and same shoulder. As a charge up, deliver a hand shiver on the offensive guard and locate the ball immediately. The defender should make sure he does not run around him. The "2" defender should go through the blocker's head and keep him away from his feet with his arms.

Diagram 2-9

(Diagram 2-10)—The tackle should not let the offensive guard hook him inside. He must move on the guard's movement and take a quick step with his outside foot, making sure he is head up on the blocker with his shoulders parallel to the line of scrimmage. The defender may have to give ground slightly so the guard will not be able to hook him. He should

Diagram 2-10

keep his arms down low to protect his "wheels" (legs) and make sure he is rid of the blocker before he totally commits himself to attacking the ball carrier.

(Diagram 2-11)—If the guard and tackle try a double team block, he must stay low and try and split the double team. Another method is to attack the post man (offensive guard); then as soon as he feels pressure, he should make an all out attack on the drive man (offensive tackle). Next, the defender should drop his outside shoulder slightly and try to wedge his shoulder between the double teaming blockers. Whirl out shallow to the line of scrimmage only as a last resort. The "2" defender should not let the blockers drive him down the line or backward. The last method to use against the double team is to drop to the knees and then rise up quickly on all fours and scramble after the ball carrier.

Diagram 2-11

(Diagram 2-12)—If the offensive guard pulls to the outside, take a set step to the inside and then take a flat pursuit course down the line of scrimmage to cut off the runner. Chart the course directly off the butt of the pulling guard. As soon as the guard pulls, think and check "trap" before getting into the pursuit course.

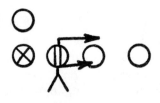

Diagram 2-12

(Diagram 2-13)—If the guard pulls to the inside, check the inside-out trap and then look for a quick inside-out step around (cross-like block) from the offensive center. The defender should take a set step when the guard blocks down, anticipating a down block by the near side offensive tackle.

Diagram 2-13

(Diagram 2-14)—If the guard blocks down and the ball goes away, trail or chase the play keeping one yard depth behind the line of scrimmage. If the passer drops back for a pull-up or sprint-out pass, use the all-out pass rush technique.

Diagram 2-14

(Diagram 2-15)—If the guard sets up for a pocket pass protection block, rush the passer in the prescribed lane. Whenever the passer drops back seven or more yards, the "2" defender should make sure to insure against the screen pass.

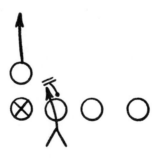

Diagram 2-15

DEFENSIVE END AND LINEBACKER "67"

Position and Alignment: Our defensive end or linebacker (67) lines up splitting the offensive end's outside foot. At times the depth and the position of alignment will change depending upon the assigned defense, down and distance. The width of the defensive end's position is dictated by the stunt called by our defensive signal caller (Diagram 2-16).

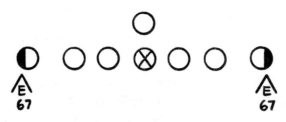

Diagram 2-16

Stance: The "67" defender lines up in a two-point stance, keeping his outside foot back so that the blocker will be unable to hook him in. The feet should be in a comfortable position, about as wide as the armpits. He should be in a football position ready to attack from the time the offensive team leaves the huddle. The end's helmet is the first key. The "67" defender should look at the near back through the end's helmet.

Responsibilities: We ask our "67" defender to perform more assignments than any other defender. To carry out all of these multi-responsibilities, he must be agile, hard-nosed, and quick.

The "67" defender must be able to stop the off tackle play. The defensive end must be able to contain the reverse, bootleg, and counter plays. He is taught to stop the sweep and never get hooked by the offensive end. In rushing the passer, he must attack from the outside in. When the sweep goes away, be ready to take a deep pursuit angle through the corner's position. He should employ the deepest pursuit angle. At times he will have to set a course for the flag. The defensive end rushes all pass actions by the quarterback including sprint passes to and away, as well as straight drop back passes.

Charge: The "67" defender must be ready to explode on the first movement of the offensive end. The charge is ignited with a short jab step with the inside foot directly into the offensive end's helmet. Make solid contact with the inside forearm blow to the opposition's base of the neck. An alternate method of contact is to use both hands, smashing the inside hand to the opponent's forehead forcing his head back; the outside hand should smash his shoulder, forcing him backward and to the inside. He should keep his thumbs in. As soon as he makes contact, he must drive at the opponent with fast, short and choppy steps.

The defender is coached to fight the pressure through the head of the blocker. Drive him back and in. If the offensive end goes to the outside to hook the defender, he should meet him and fight to the outside using his arms to keep the blocker away from his feet. Never let the end release without delivering a blow. Knock him down or at least off balance. If the offensive end drives down on the tackle, push his hips to knock him off stride. Step down to the inside to help close the off tackle hole.

The back on his side may try to take him in or out. The defender may be blocked out from the inside by a trapping guard, tackle or fullback. If he is attacked from the inside, meet the blocker with the outside foot back and anchored. Keep the body low and deliver a blow with the inside arm (same arm, same foot), attempting to stop the blocker with a strong forearm. Attack the blocker, keeping the shoulders parallel to the line of scrimmage. If the power sweep develops, keep the shoulders parallel to the line of scrimmage. If the power sweep develops, shuffle to the outside, forcing the sweep deep and to the outside. Never penetrate a yard and one-half beyond the line of scrimmage unless rushing the passer.

If the back attempts to hook the defensive end in, the defender should meet him with a forearm aimed at his chest, keeping the feet free. Never go around the blocker; always fight through his head. Remember a good defender always uses his hands. Play the blocker first and then stop the ball carrier.

Pursuit: If the ball carrier goes to the other side of the center, hold and look for a reverse, counter or bootleg; then, begin to pursue through the cornerback's position to head off the runner. Never turn your back on the ball.

Punt Rush: A punt can only be blocked by getting into the kicking line. The "67" man should set his sights on the point where the kicker will actually kick the ball, and go all out for that point. The defender must have courage to block a kick.

Pass Rush: As soon as he sees a pocket pass developing, he should rush the passer from the outside in. Expect the passer to attempt to scramble out of his pocket. Holler "Pass" as soon as you recognize a pass developing. Always rush with the arms high, forcing the passer to throw with a higher trajectory. This affords the secondary a better chance for an interception.

As the passer cocks his arm to throw, tackle him from the top down. Try to pin his arms down to his sides. The second rusher should go for the ball. As soon as the passer releases the ball, peel off to the side of the ball to be in position to block in case of an interception.

The defender should check the near back as he rushes because the back may release for a screen or flare pass. If the passer drops more than seven yards deep, read screen.

Playing the Walk-Away Position "88": Any time the offensive end is removed or split more than four yards, the defender may be assigned to drop off the line of scrimmage and split the distance between the split end and his tackle. At the last moment he may wish to move back into your forcing position (Diagram 2-17).

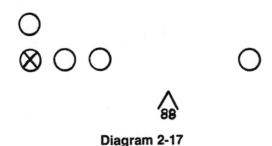

Diagram 2-17

Attack all sweeps from the outside in. On roll outs attack the quarterback. On roll outs away, attack the passer. On drop back or pocket passes, listen to the coverage call. He should support the off tackle plays to his side from the outside-in angle.

If there is a slot to his side, he should use his slot rule. He should read the near back and the ball.

DEFENSIVE END AND LINEBACKER "67" TECHNIQUE

(Diagram 2-18)—If the offensive end blocks to the inside, the defender must step down to the inside and close off the off-tackle hole. Since it is almost impossible to deliver a blow on the end who steps to the inside from the defender's position, he should push the end's outside hip with his inside hand, then immediately look for the frontside or near side back trying to block him outside. As soon as he sees the frontside back coming for him, he should make sure his shoulders are parallel to the line

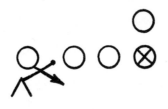

Diagram 2-18

of scrimmage and step into the blocker with his inside forearm and shoulder. The "67" defender must make sure that he dips his inside shoulder so that he is lower than the blocking back. He must hit up and through the blocker, get rid of him, and be ready to tackle the ball carrier. He must make sure he keeps his outside foot free because, if the blocker can tie up his outside foot, the ball carrier may quickly make a swing to the outside and outrun the defensive containment.

(Diagram 2-19)—The defender must make sure the offensive frontside or near back does not hook him in if the offensive end fires to the inside. As soon as he shoves the offensive end's hip, he must be ready to keep leverage on the blocking back by using his inside forearm blow on the blocker. He should keep the outside foot free and play through the head of the blocker and make the tackle.

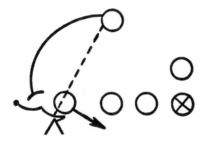

Diagram 2-19

The defender should be ready to lose ground by scalloping to the outside, but never get hooked. He should not turn his body to the inside, but keep his shoulders parallel to the line of scrimmage and make sure the outside foot is free. Once he pushes down on the offensive end, he should attack the blocking back so he has some speed and power to meet the blocker's forward momentum.

(Diagram 2-20)—When the offensive end blocks in and the fullback tries to block or kick outside, use the same technique as in Diagram 2-18. Step to the inside and deliver a forearm block through the fullback's numbers. Close the off-tackle hold, dip your inside shoulder, and keep the shoulders parallel to the goal line. When the offensive lines up in a two or three back "I," be ready for this off-tackle, fullback kick-out block.

(Diagram 2-21)—Next, the end may block in and then one of the offensive guards may attempt to trap the defender. Step in as the end blocks to the inside, check the near back, then shuffle to the inside. The

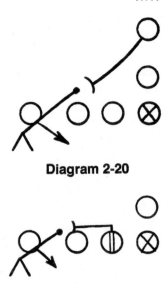

Diagram 2-20

Diagram 2-21

"67" defender is coached to dip the inside shoulder and meet the trapper with his inside shoulder. The shoulders should be parallel to the line of scrimmage. He should step to the inside with his inside foot as he delivers a blow with his inside arm. The defender should get lower than the trapper.

(Diagram 2-22)—If the end blocks in and the tackle cross blocks, the defender should shuffle down the line of scrimmage and meet the tackle

Diagram 2-22

with a forearm blow into the cross-blocking tackle's numbers. If the blocking tackle comes at the "67" defender low with his head down, the defender is coached to deliver his forearm just under the blocking tackle's helmet. Dip the shoulder and stay lower than the blocker.

(Diagram 2-23)—As soon as the end blocks in, the defender should look for the double isolation block from the frontside halfback and fullback. He may have to go down on one knee and split both of the blockers and then come up as soon as both blockers go over him. This is good once

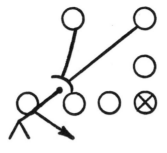

Diagram 2-23

or twice for a surprise maneuver. Normally, the defensive end must make an all-out drive straight between the blockers with his head down and blast straight at both blockers.

THE DEFENSIVE MIDDLE LINEBACKER "00"

Alignment and Position: Line up on the center's head. Usually the depth will be slightly deeper than the heels of our defensive tackle to a little over two yards off the line of scrimmage. If a short yardage play exists, we coach the middle linebacker to crowd the center. When long yardage defensive strategy exists, we teach the defensive signal caller to loosen off the line of scrimmage, so that he may give up a yard, but then he will be in excellent position to stop the long yardage play (Diagram 2-24).

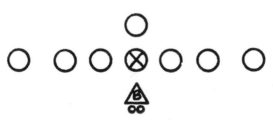

Diagram 2-24

Stance: The middle linebacker should line up in a comfortable two point stance with his feet parallel to the line of scrimmage. This balanced football position enables the linebacker to move quickly in any direction. The backer's feet should be at a comfortable width and the arms should hang down to protect the legs from the offensive blockers. The weight should be evenly distributed on the balls of the feet and his eyes should be trained on the center's helmet. As soon as the ball is snapped, the defender is taught to take a set step and then react to the center's movement. Next, he should focus his attention on the flow of the ball and take the correct pursuit course into the running lane.

Responsibilities: His immediate defensive area is from the nose of the center to the nose of the tight end's original position to each side of the center. He must be able to support any area from sideline to sideline. The middle linebacker must never get knocked off his feet. He must get rid of the center's block as soon as possible and get into his pursuit pattern. The center should never cut him off if the opposition runs a sweep or off-tackle play. If a sprint out pass develops, he must be able to cover the hook zone to the side of the sprint out.

Example of Responsibility: If the center attempts to block the middle linebacker on a play up the middle, he must devlier a blow into the blocker and fight the pressure of the block. As soon as a pulling lineman crosses his face, he should move in that direction. Once an offensive guard pulls, he should think "quick trap" first and then pursue. When a straight drop back pass develops, he should yell, "Pass," then check for the draw or screen and start back to cover his middle hook zone. If the center blocks back, the middle linebacker should take a set step and look for the quick trap.

Charge and Pursuit: On the snap of the ball, he should take a quick set step and deliver a blow into the center's chest, if the play comes directly at his position. The shoulders must be lower than the center's shoulders to provide a lift to neutralize the center's block on a quarterback sneak play. Mirror the center's movements; he is the key.

When flowing laterally pursuing the ball carrier, scallop in the direction of the play just enough to clear the line blocking. When scalloping, the first step should be with the foot to the side the linebacker is going. Keep the shoulders parallel to the line of scrimmage to be ready to meet the ball carrier head on if he cuts up into the line of scrimmage. Never overrun the sweeping ball carrier, but stay slightly behind him. The middle linebacker must be ready to hit from the time the center snaps the ball until the whistle blows to stop the action.

DEFENSIVE TECHNIQUE FOR THE MIDDLE LINEBACKER "00"

(Diagram 2-25)—If the center fires directly into the middle linebacker, he should deliver a blow on the blocker using the same arm,

Diagram 2-25

same foot. He should get rid of the blocker as soon as possible and not make it a personal duel with the offensive pivot man. At times, the defender may play the center's head with a two hand arm shiver. As soon as he hits the center with his defensive blow, he should bring both feet up parallel so he can control the blocker, releasing himself to whichever side of the blocker the ball carrier makes his cut. The middle linebacker is responsible for the draw play so he will have to be aggressive enough to control the center.

(Diagram 2-26)—If the center tries to cut off the linebacker, he should make sure the blocker does not get into his body. The middle linebacker should not permit the center to tie him up by letting the center get his head and shoulders in front of the defender, cutting him off from the ball carrier. The linebacker should scallop in the direction of the ball.

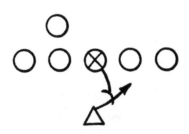

Diagram 2-26

If the center has a slight angle on the defender and is a threat to cut him off, he should go through the center's head with an inside arm lift. The ''00'' defender should step with his inside foot as he drives through the center's head with an upward, inside arm lift under the center's neck.

(Diagram 2-27)—As soon as the center sets up to block for a pocket pass, the middle linebacker should check for the draw play, then drop back into the middle hook zone. The ''00'' defender should be ready to

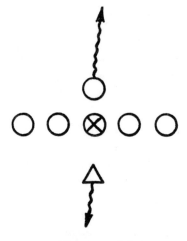

Diagram 2-27

come up once the quarterback scrambles outside of his drop back pocket and crosses the line of scrimmage.

(Diagram 2-28)—Whenever the center blocks back, the middle linebacker should take a set step in the center's direction and be ready for the tackle to block down. Look for the backside guard's quick trap and plug the middle of the line for the trap. The linebacker should deliver a blow on the blocker and keep his eyes on the ball carrier. Play the blocker's pressure by feel. Attack the ball carrier on a quick trap, right now!

Diagram 2-28

DEFENSIVE OUTSIDE LINEBACKER "66"

Alignment and Position: The defensive linebacker should line up head on the offensive end or head up on his original position whenever there is a split end to that side. The usual depth will be slightly deeper than the heels of the defensive end. Crowd the end versus short yardage strategy and loosen when long yardage strategy dictates (Diagram 2-29).

Diagram 2-29

Stance: Use a parallel two point stance to be able to move in any direction. The feet should be a comfortable width with the outside foot slightly staggered in a heel to toe relationship. The arms should hang down ready to protect the legs, and the knees should be slightly bent. The weight should be on the balls of the feet and the eyes should be focused on the end's helmet. The defender must be ready to move on movement and react to the end's or the tackle's move and then quickly pick up the backfield flow. Once the offensive end releases, blocks, or sets up to pass block, the defender should quickly check the offensive tackle's movement.

Responsibilities: If the sprint out pass comes his way, he should normally attack the passer. The attack route will depend upon the defender's alignment, the offensive set, and the defensive call. The "66" defender is the contain man on power sweeps. Key the nearest blocker's helmet and never let the ball get outside. If the end blocks out and the tackle blocks down, he must be ready to stuff the isolation play. If the blocking offensive back comes directly at the defender, he should make sure he gets lower than the blocker does. (Don't wait for the isolation blocker; attack him!)

Example of Responsibility: The "66" defender must play head up on the wide man against a tight wing or tight slot formation. He must never get hooked in by the wide blocker. On all off-tackle maneuvers, he should attack the ball carrier using an outside-in angle. The assigned man on option plays will vary from week to week and will depend upon whether there is a lead back involved. It is most important that the "66" defender and the defensive end communicate with each other pertaining to the particular assigned offensive man. When the quarterback drops directly back for a pocket pass, the linebacker's assignment is to cover the hook zone to his side, if there is a tight end to his side. If there is a split end to his side, he will be assigned to cover the curl pass on all back up or drop back passes.

Charge and Pursue: The ''66'' defender must be ready to move on movement and deliver a blow into the first offensive man who attempts to block him. Then, he must be ready to fight pressure and get into his correct pursuit course. Next, be ready to gang tackle the ball carrier. The second man to reach the ball carrier is coached to go for the ball and force the fumble.

DEFENSIVE TECHNIQUES FOR THE DEFENSIVE OUTSIDE LINEBACKER "66"

(Diagram 2-30)—If the offensive end tries to hook the linebacker in, he should fight to the outside and look for the quick pitch. Go through the end's head rather than making too wide an arc to open up the funnel for the ball carrier to make his break. The ''66'' defender should key the triangle in which the base is the offensive tackle and end, and the top of the triangle is the frontside running back.

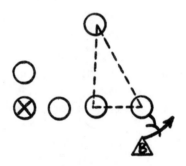

Diagram 2-30

(Diagram 2-31)—When the end blocks straight on the linebacker, he must deliver a blow on the end with his inside forearm, then fight through

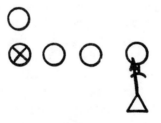

Diagram 2-31

the head of the blocker. Make sure the end does not release clean off the line of scrimmage for a pass. If the end tries to block the linebacker outside, the defender should fight the blocker's pressure and attack the ball carrier. He should go directly through the head of the blocker.

(Diagram 2-32)—The linebacker should read the tackle, and as soon as the end and tackle block down, he must attack the off-tackle play from an outside-in angle. On an option play, he must be assigned to tackle the quarterback or crash to the inside and tackle the dive man. The option assignment will vary from game to game and will depend upon the stunt called by one defensive captain. If the tackle tries to block the linebacker to the outside, he should meet the blocker with his inside forearm and then fight through the blocker's head.

Diagram 2-32

(Diagram 2-33)—If the tight end and tackle set up to pass block, the "66" defender should drop back into the hook zone. If the linebacker is

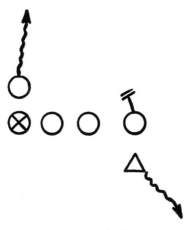

Diagram 2-33

in his "66" position to the split end's side, he should key the offensive
tackle. If the tackle sets up to pass block and the quarterback sets up in a
back up pocket pass, he is now assigned to drop back into the curl zone,
checking for the movement of the split end.

(Diagram 2-34)—When the tight end blocks to his outside and the
offensive tackle blocks to his inside, the linebacker should quickly step up

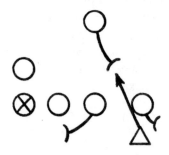

Diagram 2-34

and plug the off-tackle hole. As he fills the hole, he should look for the
near back on his isolation blocking course. The outside linebacker should
meet power with power and be ready to hit the ball carrier as soon as the
defender gets rid of the blocking back. If two backs come at him at the
same time, he must get lower than the blockers and go down low and then
up, trying to split the two blockers.

Chapter 3

Forty Defense Stunts

COACHING STUNTS

Before we use any stunt, we explain to our players the reasons for using a particular stunt. We also explain the time, place, and against what basic offensive formations we will use this stunt and when to call it off. Then the defensive staff explains the strong and weak points of this stunt. All of our defenders are taught that there is no magic about successfully stunting against an opponent, but it is the technique employed by the defensive stunting team that makes the gaming stunt successful.

The blitzing linebacker or stunting lineman is never told to just "go." He is taught techniques to use to get to the ball as quickly as possible. Dropping the shoulder, head and shoulder fake, leveling off, spinning, picking up grass, arm action, hand and eye fakes, blitzing path, secondary blitzing path, etc., are all explained before we ever turn our red dogging or stunting defender loose.

JUMPING AND STUNTING DEFENSES

The moving or jumping defense gives the defense an advantage by:

1. Confusing the offensive blockers and making them indecisive as to whom to block.
2. Forcing the offense to adjust their count to a quick or late count.
3. Confusing the quarterback as to which direction he should focus his running or short passing attack.
4. Cutting down the offensive splits. If the offense does not cut down the size of their splits, the defense will fire through these open areas at will.

5. Moving their strength to the offensive strength at the last moment.

6. The fact that it is more difficult to block a moving defender than a stationary defender.

DEFENSIVE NUMBERED STUNTS OFF THE 40 DEFENSE

Defensively, we number our stunts by numbering our linebackers. Against two tight ends in our normal 40 Defense, we number our three linebackers from right to left 1-2-3 (Diagram 3-1).

Diagram 3-1

Against a split end formation, we number our three linebackers with "1" always to the split end side; the next linebacker (middle linebacker) is "2" and the linebacker to the tight end side is "3" (Diagram 3-2 and 3-3).

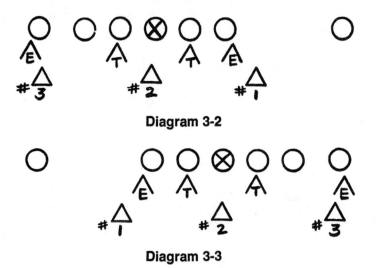

Diagram 3-2

Diagram 3-3

If our defensive middle linebacker calls "40," the defense would line up just as in Diagram 3-2, if the offensive lined up with a split end to the defensive right. The defense would then play their normal 40 reactions as the ball was put into play.

When we wish to stunt the defensive outside linebacker, we merely add a number to our 40 Defense. If we called "41," our "1" linebacker would blitz in the manner shown in Diagram 3-4. The other four defensive members of our seven man front play their regular 40 assignments.

41 CALL

Diagram 3-4

The "1" linebacker would fire through the "3" gap, while the right end would step into the offensive left tackle's shoulder trying to draw his block. The defensive end (45) would then step to the outside and have outside defensive responsibility. The defensive right tackle would line up in his regular "2" alignment and then shoot into the "1" gap. The "2" man is taught to take a quick lateral step with his inside foot and then a quick crossover step with his inside foot. If the offensive right guard would attempt to shoot his head across to cut off the "2" man's path, the defender is taught to bring his right arm up and through the blocker's neck. This technique is accomplished by throwing the same arm (right) and same step (right crossover) at the same time. As soon as the defensive tackle hits the "1" gap, he must have his shoulders parallel to the line of scrimmage and be ready to meet a quick-hitting ball carrier immediately. If the ball goes to his right or left, the defensive tackle must be ready to dip his shoulder in the direction of the flow and take a flat course to cut off the ball carrier.

The firing linebacker's (1) technique is similar to the defensive tackle's because he must hit the "3" gap, keeping his shoulders parallel to the line of scrimmage until he locates the ball.

The defensive coaching staff teaches each linebacker the grass drill. This drill teaches the linebacker to scallop along the line and then fire into a designated area. Once the linebacker hits his spot, the coach points a right or left direction and the linebacker must cut to his right or left and pick up a blade of grass with his right hand (if right is the direction the coach signals). This forces the linebacker to dip the shoulder in the direction he is going, which puts him in a good hitting position to ward off an opponent's block from the same direction the linebacker is heading (Diagram 3-4).

The 42 call tells both of our tackles to fire into the "1" gap to their side, using the same parallel step technique previously discussed for the tackle in our 41 stunt. The middle linebacker then is assigned to blitz through the "3" gap to the tight end's side. Whenever the offense attacks the area to their tight end's side, the middle linebacker (2 linebacker) is able to meet the thrust head on. The "2" linebacker is also often successful in running down the wide plays and sprint out passer from the backside. If the play is a drop back pass, the middle linebacker continues through with his 42 stunt. This defensive blitz often confuses the offensive guards' and center's blocking assignments. The semi-delayed attack by the middle linebacker often blitzes him free into the opponent's backfield (Diagram 3-5).

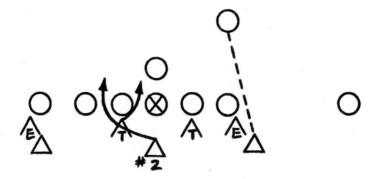

42 CALL

Diagram 3-5

The 43 call sends the "3" linebacker through the "5" gap, while the defensive left end is taught to draw the offensive right end's block. Then the defensive end is assigned to step to his outside to protect against the quick pitch or the sweep toward the defensive left end. The other five members of the front seven play their normal 40 assignments and are not affected by the "3" blitz (Diagram 3-6).

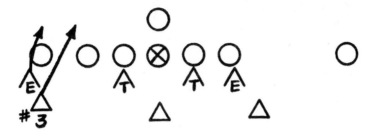

43 CALL

Diagram 3-6

When the defensive signal caller wants all three of the linebackers to blitz, he simply says, "40 All." This call means a "41" to the right defensive end, right defensive tackle, and right linebacker, a "42" to the middle linebacker and left defensive tackle, and a "43" to the left end and left linebacker (Diagram 3-7).

40 ALL CALL

Diagram 3-7

If the defensive signal caller wants all of the linebackers to blitz, but through difficult areas, he just calls, "40 All Switch" (Diagram 3-8). The switch means that the defenders change their stunting patterns. The outside linebackers exchange their stunts with the defensive ends and the middle linebacker exchanges his stunts with the defensive tackles.

40 ALL SWITCH CALL

Diagram 3-8

Against two tight ends, the 40 All Switch would look like it is drawn in Diagram 3-9. The middle linebacker would then be assigned a key (possibly the offensive fullback), who would direct him to one of the two open gaps as shown in Diagram 3-9.

40 ALL SWITCH CALL

Diagram 3-9

Depending upon the specific game strategy, the defense could hold the defensive middle linebacker, enabling him to play a particular draw play on a given down by just playing regular. To do this, the signal caller would simply call "41-43," which would blitz the two outside linebackers. This would leave the middle linebacker playing his normal assignment so he could be free to zero in on the draw (Diagram 3-10).

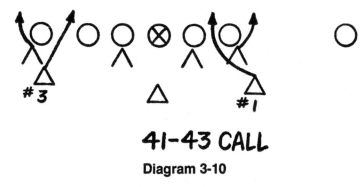

41-43 CALL

Diagram 3-10

If the defense wanted to assign the weakside or the number 1 linebacker a particular man to man assignment on an expected passing down and still blitz two linebackers, the defensive quarterback would just call, "42 and 43." This call would blitz the "2" and "3" linebackers both to the strong side and leave the "1" linebacker in his normal assignment so he could play the halfback in a man to man assignment. This would enable the safetyman to the weak side to be free to roam as a free safetyman in a man to man pass defensive call (Diagram 3-11).

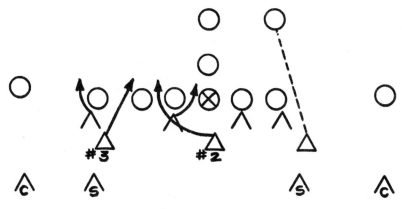

Diagram 3-11

Whenever we want to rush our ends from an outside-in angle, we simply call "Wide go," which rushes our two ends. These ends are taught to aim their rushes at the outside foot of the halfback's normal set position (Diagram 3-12). When we want both ends and outside linebacker to go, we simply give a "Wide double go" call which assigns both of our ends and linebackers to blitz from their outside-in angles (Diagram 3-13).

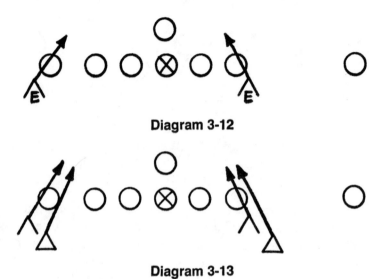

Diagram 3-12

Diagram 3-13

Chapter 4

Forty Defense
Teaching Philosophy

Our basic teaching philosophy is to use one basic defense, the Forty Defense, and then adjust from the basic defense to a variety of different forty-looks. After we show our Forty Defense, a specific offensive formation or powerful offensive personnel may force us to adjust to a Forty Bubble, Pro Forty, Split Forty, or Stack Forty Defense. We first teach each player the overall concept of each defense, and then we teach each player his particular technique and fit each technique and assignment into the whole defense. This is our whole-part-whole teaching method.

TEACHING THE BASICS

It is not how well the defensive staff knows the basic defense, but rather how well they can teach it to their defensive players that makes a great defense. The defensive coaches should never over-estimate an opponent so that the defenders loose their confidence, nor should the coach underestimate the opposition so that the defenders become overconfident. The defensive staff should go back to their basic defense and actually subtract some of their defensive assignment whenever the defense begins to loose its effectiveness. Our defensive motto in this situation is to "go back to the basics."

MOTIVATING DEFENSIVE PLAYERS

The coach should occasionally stop practice and applaud or pat the back of a defender who has made a hard hit. The defensive coach may splice particularly hard hits on films for a special "stingers" or "head hunters" reel. A Big Hit Play Chart may list the players's name and picture of the best hit of each game. Players are motivated by setting the defensive goals high, but not so high that they cannot obtain these goals. In drills a particularly hard hit should be applauded by the entire squad. Players are often motivated during off the field talks by their position coaches. Person to person meetings in the football office, at lunch, after practice, or at the student union often pay off in helping to motivate players to bigger and better all-out efforts. A personal coach-player viewing of the films is most helpful to many individual players. The coach should let the player do most of the talking. Football coaches who are the most successful motivators are also good listeners.

BELIEVING IN THE DEFENSE

All defenders and the coaching staff must firmly believe that the defensive organization will win. This must be a positive approach by all players through the development of pride and concentration concerning all defensive assignments and techniques. The overall defensive philosophy must be one of attack. The defense must pressure the offense into making physical and mental offensive mistakes. Defensive quickness and agility are the most important attributes for any defender. The coach must know the defense he is teaching completely. He must believe in the defense and sell the defense to the players. If the coach does not believe in the total defensive program, he cannot expect the players to believe in the defense.

ENTHUSIASTIC APPROACH

A team plays just like it is coached. An enthusiastic and aggressive defense reflects the coach's personality. The defensive coach can be just as tough as he desires as long as his players believe he is fair, and in turn will back them up whenever they are in need of help. The coach must make his players understand that all of the drills, conditioning, and coaching will make each individual defender a better player. The coach must demand the very best from all players. He must instill pride, desire, and enthusiasm into all of the defenders by reflecting these important attributes in his personality. If the defensive unit can build the tempo of hustling and strong conditioning in the latter stages of the practice sessions, they will be able to pick up the game tempo in the all-important fourth quarter.

COACHING DRILLS

The drill should resemble closely an actual phase of the game itself. A good coach will always explain the "why" or the purpose of a particular drill. Therefore, we try to explain, demonstrate, or view the entire picture on film so that the player is able to visualize how his individual assignment or technique fits into the whole defense scheme. Once the player is able to understand his role in the defensive drill, the more meaningful the total picture becomes to the individual and the team.

Each drill emphasizes a specific phase of how a player should react to a particular offensive maneuver. If a player can react quickly with a reflex action, it is easier for him to adjust to a sudden offensive technique or play. The drill is set up so that the player gains the correct mental and physical poise and confidence of the game-like reaction of "I have been here before" feeling. Therefore, in each drill a player should use the same technique he will use in the game.

SELECTING AND COACHING THE DEFENSIVE TACKLES "2"

The defensive tackles should be our two biggest, strongest, and toughest linemen. These two defenders are the anchors of our defense. Since their alignment is head up or at times slightly outside of the down offensive opponent, they must be taught to read the head of this defender. Our two anchoring linemen must be ready to react in any direction if their offensive key pulls to the right or the left; therefore, their defensive stance must be balanced, in order to shuffle to the left or the right while reading the head of the opposing lineman.

If the opposing lineman blocks directly at our defensive tackle, he uses number blocking or "high blocking" techniques. If the blocker uses the scramble or "low blocking" technique going for the defensive tackle's legs, the defender is taught to use his hands, utilizing his hand shiver technique. The hands help to keep the blocker away from the defender's legs. We also teach our defender to push down on the blocker's helmet, forcing the blocker's head into the ground. One alternative defensive technique employed by our anchoring tackle is to place his hands on the blocker's shoulder as he begins to scramble, and then the defender is taught to leapfrog over the blocker's head and attack the ball carrier. This technique is an excellent surprise maneuver.

These are the same techniques we teach to our defensive ends whenever they are playing in their four point positions in our Pro Forty Defense. All of our down defenders must not only be strong but must also be quick to be able to read, deliver a blow, and pursue the ball carrier. Whenever play goes away, our end is usually assigned the task to trail the ball carrier.

DEFENSIVE TACKLE "2"

The defensive tackles must anchor the defense and read the movement of the offensive guards. Since these defenders are head up and in a four point stance, we coach them to read the hand of the offensive guards. If these head up defensive tackles are quick in their lateral movement, we may minimize the necessity of size at the defensive tackle position (Diagram 4-1).

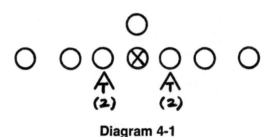

Diagram 4-1

Keying and reading the offensive blocking patterns is carried on throughout the season. This can be best taught using these five on two drills (Diagram 4-2).

Diagram 4-2

The execution of the defensive tackle is to take a lateral step with the foot nearest the direction indicated by the offensive blocker's head. Whip the blocker using the same forearm and same step in the direction of the blocker's helmet. If the blocker drives straight at the defender attempting to execute a snoot or numbers block, the defender is taught to use a forearm shiver directly at the defender. There may be a time when we ask the defensive tackle to use a submarine technique by going down and up. This means the defender will shoot low under the blocker's legs and then come up as soon as possible.

DEFENSIVE TACKLE DRILLS (FORTY DEFENSE)

We teach the submarine techniques, previously mentioned, in our Submarine-Crab Drill (Diagram 4-3).

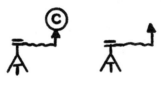

Diagram 4-3

Two other drills which have helped our defensive tackle's quickness reactions have been our Move on Movement Drill (Diagram 4-4) and the Flat Course Drill (Diagram 4-5).

Diagram 4-4

Submarine Crab Drill

Objective: React after submarine technique and scramble on all fours.

Organization: Two defensive tackles, one coach and a football. Two defenders assume their normal alignment.

Execution: On the snap of the ball, the two defensive tackles submarine

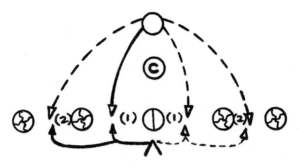

Diagram 4-5

and use a belly slam. Then they quickly get into a four point crabbing position on the wave of the ball by the coach. The coach then flips the ball on the ground for the tackles to recover the fumble.

Coaching points: Teaches quick recovery from submarine charge and teaches crabbing reaction to the way. Defender is forced to stay low throughout the drill (Diagram 4-3).

Move On Movement Drill

Objective: Quick feet, stepping in the correct direction with the correct foot.

Organization: One on one. Defender lines head up and shades outside shoulder.

Execution: (a) Fire Out—Blocker fires straight and defender may step with either foot and is coached to use his forearm shiver.

(b) Cut Off—Blocker attempts a cut off block and defender steps with the right foot first and the left foot second. Defender must key the blocker's feet and head. Short right step in cut off direction and the left foot should step across in the same direction.

(c) Reach—Blocker attempts to reach block and the defender first takes a quick short left lead step with left foot to reach side. The backside right foot steps across in the same direction.

Coaching Points: Defender must protect the second backside step in both the cut off and reach block with a swing uppercut technique with the backside arm. This arm often gets up under the defender's pads, straightening up the blocker, and minimizing his charge (Diagram 4-4).

Flat Course Drill "2"

Objective: Defensive tackle maintains a flat course along the line of scrimmage and attacks the ball carrier with shoulders parallel to the line of scrimmage.

Organization: Five stand-up dummies, coach, ball carrier, football and one defensive tackle.

Execution: Coach hands the ball off to a runner who runs into the defensive "1" or cuts outside to the defensive "3" gap. On the snap of the ball, the defender delivers a blow and then takes a flat pursuit course to the ball. Defensive tackle is coached to keep his shoulders square to the line of scrimmage and make full speed tackle on ball carrier.

Coaching points: Maintain a good football position on the approach and make good head-on tackle with the shoulders squared to the line of scrimmage (Diagram 4-5).

SELECTING AND COACHING THE DEFENSIVE ENDS "67"

The defensive ends must be quick enough to put pressure on the passer and be able to contain the outside plays. They must be big and strong enough to be able to stop the power off-tackle play. At times the defensive end must move into a four point stance and line up in a "45" position (outside shoulder of the offensive tackle) and be ready to fight against the offensive end and tackle's power double team block. Therefore when we select a defensive end, we look for a strong, rangy, quick defender who can play from both the two and the four point stance.

DEFENSIVE END'S PLAY RESPONSIBILITY "67" OR "45"

In the previous chapters as well as this chapter, we have stressed the defender's responsibility versus the offensive blocking patterns. Along with teaching how to attack these blocks, we also include specific offensive plays we must stop each week during the season; therefore, we add additional blockers, fakers, and the ball carrier to group and half line drills and scrimmages for our defense.

The defensive end's key is the near back through the offensive end to the tight end side. The key is the near back through the offensive tackle to the split side. As soon as the ball is snapped, the defensive end must read the quarterback immediately along with his other two keys (Diagram 4-6).

The defensive end is responsible to stop the off-tackle play by squeezing down from his outside-in angle. He must be ready to tackle the quarterback on the option play (tight end's side), force the sweep, contain the quick pitch, rush the drop back quarterback from the outside-in angle,

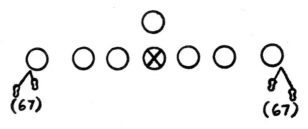

Diagram 4-6

contain the roll or sprint out pass, and take the correct pursuit course to cut off the ball carrier. If the play goes away, the defensive end to the tight end's side must chase and look for a counter maneuver.

It is also most important to coach the defensive end to aim for a specific spot. The spot will move slightly to the inside if the offensive end blocks down to his inside, but we show the defender a spot approximately one and one-half yards deep directly over the tight end's original position[1] (Diagram 4-7). Thus, the defensive end is coached to shuffle to that spot from his "67" alignment as quickly as possible. Then we teach him the technique he must use to stop a particular off-tackle kick-out block or how to play cat and mouse versus the triple optioning quarterback.

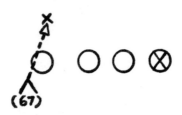

Diagram 4-7

As soon as an option play develops, the defensive end should go to his point and then play cat and mouse with the quarterback (Diagram 4-8). If the quarterback pitches quickly, the defensive end must be ready to shuffle out and head off the ball carrier (Diagram 4-9). If a force call is assigned, the defensive end is coached to attack the quarterback now! He is taught to tackle the quarterback high, around the shoulders, and use the

---

[1]*Coaching Note:* The reason the author noted the spot as "approximately" one and one-half yards deep is that if the blocker attempts to kick or block the end out, the defensive end is taught not to penetrate. But if the defender attacks a sweep, the one and one-half yard penetration will force the sweeping ball carrier to go deeper and wider and will help to delay and take away the effectiveness of the sweep.

outside hand to block or bat the potential pitch by the optioning quarter-back (Diagram 4-10).

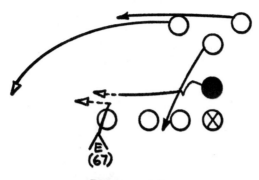

Diagram 4-8

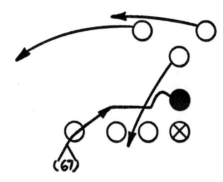

Diagram 4-9

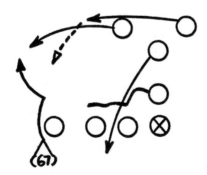

(67) MUST MAKE PITCH MAN TURN UP
TO THE INSIDE

Diagram 4-10

Against the sprint out pass, the defensive end is coached to gain depth and contain the sprint out or roll out. This means the defensive end must first go to his spot and then take a picture of the play. As soon as the blocker's head attempts to hook or go outside of the defensive end's body, the defender must use his hands and shuffle to the outside and attack the passer from an outside-in angle (Diagram 4-11).

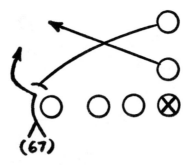

Diagram 4-11

All of the opposition's favorite plays are practiced in the individual defensive drill against an offensive skeleton unit. This is the type of individualized coaching that builds championship defensive teams.

DEFENSIVE END DRILLS (FORTY DEFENSE)

The defensive end must be able to shed blockers and maintain leverage on the ball carrier. Therefore, we emphasize two drills in our practice sessions which teach getting rid of the offensive reach blocking and head-on blocking techniques. The Defensive Leverage Drill (Diagram 4-12) and Shed Drill (Diagram 4-13) are set up to destroy the blocker and attack the ball carrier. The third drill we feature continually in our drill sessions for our defensive ends is the correct technique of playing the option. The Option Drill (Diagram 4-14) teaches the defender how to play the cat and mouse technique against an offensive skeleton unit.

Defensive Leverage Drill

Objective: Maintain leverage on the offensive sweep play.

Organization: Four players on offense, three playing the role of blockers and one ball carrier versus one defender.

Execution: The defender should shuffle to the outside using his forearm shiver to keep the blockers away from his feet. The defender should keep

Diagram 4-12

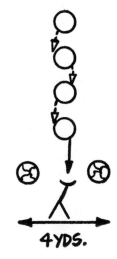

4YDS.

Diagram 4-13

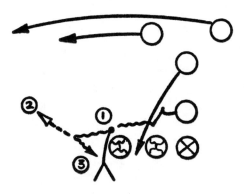

Diagram 4-14

his eyes on the blocker and may lose some ground backward to maintain outside leverage. Once the defender gets rid of the last blocker, he should take the correct pursuit course for the ball carrier. As the defender sheds each blocker, he must remember to keep his elbows locked and push off the defender's helmet and shoulders as he maintains leverage on the ball carrier.

Coaching Points: The defender must make sure he has completely gotten rid of the blocker before he takes on the next blocker (Diagram 4-12).

Shed Drill

Objective: Teach defender how to shed blockers and react to the ball carrier.

Organization: Five offensive players in a straight row sprinting at a defender in rapid action. Defender attacks blocker two yards away from first offensive player with two dummies four yards apart as boundaries. Coach stands to one side of the offensive line with a football.

Execution: Defender takes his normal stance and moves on the offensive player's movement. The defender is taught to shed each blocker and look for the ball carrier. The ball carrier is designated by the coach, who slips the ball to any one of the five offensive players.

Coaching Points: Teaches the defender to shed the blocker with the backside hand, away from the arm delivering the blow. Makes the defender react to the ball carrier and assume a good football hitting position. Do not overextend the body while attacking the blocker (Diagram 4-13).

Option Drill "67"

Objective: Force the quarterback to keep the ball. Cat and mouse technique.

Organization: Line up offensive end and backfield.

Execution: Offense runs the triple option and the defender is coached to get depth and make the quarterback keep the ball. The defender must shuffle along the line just over one arm's length from the offensive quarterback. Must remain in a position to get back to tackle the quarterback (inside-out angle) or take the correct angle and attack the pitchman (outside-in angle).

Coaching Points: Defender must be coached to shuffle parallel to the line of scrimmage with his shoulders squared so he can attack the inside or the outside ball carrier (Diagram 4-14).

SELECTING AND COACHING
THE MIDDLE LINEBACKER "00"

The middle linebacker should line up head on the center approximately two yards off the ball, depending upon down and distance tendencies. His two point stance should be a balanced, low football position. His shoulders should be parallel to the line of scrimmage. The middle linebacker's key should be the quarterback looking through the center's head. The middle linebacker should not only be the top defender, but he is also the defensive captain who is assigned the duties of calling our defensive signals. He must be agile enough to play an offensive running back man to man on certain pass plays, and strong enough to destroy the center's block and attack the ball carrier. At times he may not only be assigned to defeat the center's block, but the defensive tackle may also attempt to double team block him with his offensive center. He must be able to meet the quick trap head-on as soon as the center blocks to one side or the other. As soon as he reads the center's frontside or backside block, he must be ready to fill the middle, looking for a trapping linemen or a back or backs on an isolating course.

MIDDLE LINEBACKER'S STANCE "00"

The middle linebacker should line up in a two point stance, with his legs bent in a 45 degree angle, ready to uncoil on the first offensive blocker who challenges the linebacker. The head should be up and the butt should be down. The feet should be approximately parallel, with the body weight evenly distributed on the balls of the feet. His arms should hang relaxed, slightly forward of the thighs, with the hands inside of the knees (Diagram 4-15).

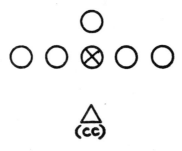

Diagram 4-15

EXECUTION AND INITIAL MOVEMENT

The "00" defender should react to the center's head. If the center attempts to block the middle linebacker, he should be taught to destroy the center's block with the forearm or shiver, reading the center's block and the direction of the ball. If the middle linebacker should ever be cut off, he should correct his position with a deeper pursuit angle.

The middle linebacker has two reads:

(1) Quick Read—If the near back comes directly at the middle linebacker, he must play the blocker tough and shed him and make the tackle.

(2) Slow Read—When the backs go in opposite directions of each other, the middle linebacker should stay at home, step up, meet the blocker with a bold forearm or shiver, find the ball, and then take the correct pursuit angle.

RESPONSIBILITIES

The middle linebacker is responsible for the draw play. Play the play action pass for the run first and the pass second. Scallop down the line of scrimmage and always be ready to meet the ball carrier with shoulders parallel to the goal line. He should be coached to meet the screen from an inside-out angle. The depth of the middle linebacker should be adjusted depending upon the down, distance, and game siutations.

MIDDLE LINEBACKER ELIMINATES
INTERIOR SPLITS WITH A CALL

Whenever the opponent's offense begins to use maximum or wide splits, particularly between the offensive center and guard area, we minimize these splits with a call by our middle linebacker. The middle linebacker is coached to call the defensive tackle's first name whenever the guard's split moves the defensive tackle too far away from his original position. Therefore, as soon as the tackle hears his first name, he immediately jumps into the guard-center gap to his side and uses his penetrating gap charge. The middle linebacker is now responsible to quickly scrape off past the tackle's new position, if flow shows toward the gap tackle's area (Diagram 4-16).

Another defensive technique the middle linebacker is taught to eliminate the offensive guard's maximum splits is to automatically call a

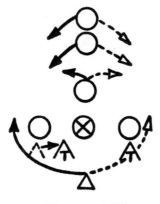

Diagram 4-16

gap stack to the side of the maximum split. Therefore, this defense would end up in our 40 Stack Defense (Diagram 4-17).[2]

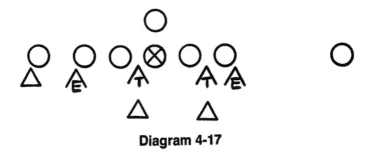

Diagram 4-17

MIDDLE LINEBACKER DRILLS (FORTY DEFENSE)

The Triple Explosion Drill (Diagram 4-18) teaches the defender to react to blockers from either side as well as the head-on blocker from the offensive center. Our Quick-Slow Read Drill (Diagram 4-19a and 4-19b) teaches the middle linebacker how to read the different offensive back-field maneuvers. The Seven Man Hit and Spin Drill (Diagram 4-20) is used in the majority of our practice sessions to teach the linebackers a good forearm, how to spin off the blocker, and gather up and continue this sequence after skipping one dummie.

[2]The 40 Stack Defense is discussed and illustrated in Chapters 2 and 3.

TRIPLE EXPLOSION DRILL

Diagram 4-18

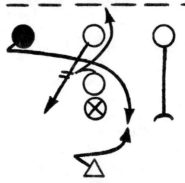

FAST READ DRILL

SLOW READ

Diagram 4-19

HIT AND SPIN DRILL

Diagram 4-20

Triple Explosion Drill

Objective: Deliver a blow to the side of the blocker; emphasize same arm, same foot.

Organization: Three men playing the role of offensive blockers. Coach stands behind the defender.

Execution: Three men line up in a triangular alignment facing the defender in a two point stance with the coach behind the defender. The two outside defenders line up one yard outside the defender's shoulders and the middle blocker lines up nose on the defender one yard away from the defender. On the signal by the coach, one of the blockers attacks the defender. The defender delivers a forearm blow using the arm to the side of the blocker. The defender steps with the same side foot. The step should be a short step accompanied by an explosive blow. As soon as the defender hits the blocker, he is coached to quickly return to his two point stance, in a football position ready to hit the next blocker. After five repetitions, the coach calls "change" and the defender becomes the right side blocker and all other members of the group rotate their positions in a clockwise rotation.

Coaching Points: Coach signals blockers by hand so defender moves on movement of offensive man rather than sound. This is a more realistic defensive game-like reaction (Diagram 4-18).

Quick-Slow Read Linebacker Drill

Objective: Teach the linebacker to distinguish between a quick and slow read and to improve defensive reactions to the ball carrier.

Organization: Line up a three or four man backfield and run plays to help the linebacker to read. The linebacker should line up in his usual alignments and about two and one-half yards off the line of scrimmage.

Execution: The linebacker should react to the fast read of all the backs going in the same direction, by stepping up and into the line of scrimmage. The defender should step into the point of attack and butt or jolt the ball carrier (Diagram 4-19a). The slow read consists of the fullback attacking one side of the center, and the two halfbacks going toward the point of attack on the opposite side of the center (Diagram 4-19b). This drill forces the linebacker to redirect his key and his movement from one area to another area. He must take a picture of the complete play and not overcommit himself to the first movement of the opposition's back. This drill forces the linebacker to maintain a low base.

Coaching Points: Linebacker must move quickly, stepping up and to the point of attack. Shed the blocker and make the tackle.

  Seven Man Hit and Spin Drill

Objective: Defender delivers good forearm and spins out low and deep and attacks the sled again.

Organization: Hit every other pad of the seven man sled.

Execution: Defenders line up in single file and are coached to deliver a forearm on the first pad and then reverse out in a 360 degree turn, on all fours, and then step up and hit the third pad. Skip every other pad and step up with the same foot, same forearm blast.

Coaching Points: Defender must spin out deep so he is able to attack the sled with his shoulders parallel to the seven man sled. The spin out should be used on all fours. Short choppy steps should be stressed (Diagram 4-20).

COACHING LINEBACKER'S SHEDDING TECHNIQUES
(Diagram 4-21)

Most of the shedding by the linebacker is done low with the hands and arms to keep the offensive blockers away from the scalloping linebacker's feet. The scalloping linebacker should work his way down the line of scrimmage keeping his shoulders parallel to the line of scrimmage. He should always go through the head of the blocker and never go behind the potential blocker. If the forearm smash is used, the other arm must be kept free in order to steer the blocker away from his path.

The shedding linebacker should meet the blocker with his outside foot whenever the blocker is attacking from an outside-in angle. The defender should stay low so that only a small part of his body is exposed. His low body area enables his arms and hands to protect his legs from the

Diagram 4-21

blockers. He should make sure he stays on the ball carrier's hip so the ball carrier will not be able to cut back against the grain and make the long gainer.

The scalloping and shedding defender must be able to read the blocking pattern of the offensive attack. If the opposition attempts to use a back blocking on an "iso" or torpedo type block, the linebacker must be ready to shoot right into the hole and attack the back and plug up the hole.

SELECTING AND COACHING THE STRONG OUTSIDE LINEBACKERS "66"

The strong side linebacker must be agile and quick enough to force contain the outside sweep to his side. He must also be strong enough to attack the tackle-end seam whenever the offense directs the point of the attack to the off-tackle hole to his side.

Whenever our strong side linebacker attacks the off-tackle hole, he must first look for a lineman blocking out on him from a regular frontside and backside pulling position. Next, he should look for a back ready to block him. If the back attempts to block him out, the linebacker must be ready to squeeze the play to the inside by attacking the blocker. He must keep his shoulders parallel to the line of scrimmage and meet the blocker from an outside-in angle, delivering an inside forearm blow and stepping with the inside foot. If the quarterback fakes the ball and sets up for a play action pass, the linebacker must adjust his course and rush the passer with his arms high.

STRONG SIDE LINEBACKER

The strong side linebacker must be the toughest and strongest of the linebacker corps. He must be strong enough to handle the tight end and stop the off-tackle power plays and quick enough to defend against the flat, hook, or curl passes.

Stance: The linebacker should use a balanced two point stance with the arms hanging relaxed just inside his knees. We do not want the strong side linebacker flexing his knees too much because he will be unable to move quickly from this overly crouched stance.

Alignment: The strong side linebacker is taught to line up head-up or just to the inside foot of the tight end (Diagram 4-22). If these are two tight ends and the ball is in the middle of the field, he should always line up on the defensive left side.

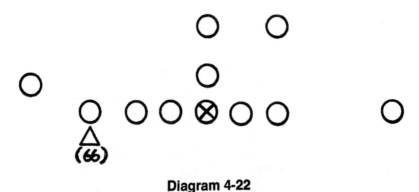

Diagram 4-22

Key: Key the tight end and tackle.

Read: Read the blocking pattern of the tight end and the offensive tackle on the move. Then pick up the blocking pattern of the near side offensive back or a pulling lineman blocking from an inside-out angle.

Coaching Point: Never let the tight end block the linebacker inside or screen him to the inside.

Responsibility: The linebacker should stop the run first and the pass second. The strong side linebacker must be ready to play the off-tackle hole. Normally on a triple or belly option play, the strong side linebacker is responsible for the dive man on a Forty Defense; therefore, he must be responsible to stop the inside plays first and the outside maneuvers second. He must keep his shoulders parallel to the line of scrimmage and take on the near side blocking back head-on and fight pressure with pressure. The outside linebacker has time to give ground slightly, to get rid of a blocker and still recover to tackle the ball carrier.

If the ball carrier goes away, the strong linebacker is coached to chug the tight end and keep him outside. Drop back slowly and look for a counter or reverse action, cushion, locate the ball, and then take the correct angle of pursuit.

If a sprint out pass develops toward the outside linebacker and he has a predetermined blitz call, attack the quarterback on an outside-in angle and tackle him from the head down. He should keep his arms high and make the passer throw over the outstretched arms. If the strong side linebacker is playing normal, he must be ready to drop back to his pass responsibility on a forty-five degree angle. The linebacker must keep his eyes on the quarterback and maintain an outside position on the sprinting passer and be ready to attack the passer once he decides to run.

If the passer executes a straight drop back pass, the outside linebacker is coached to sprint back to the outside flat and square his shoulders up as soon as the passer sets up in the pocket. (No deep back is assigned to the strong side flat zone.)

SELECTING AND COACHING THE WEAK OUTSIDE LINEBACKER

The weak outside linebacker is usually lined up to the split end side. He has many of the same responsibilities as the strong side outside linebacker, only he usually has more defensive pass assignment responsibilities. He has more of a force-contain responsibility against the sweep but may also be assigned a flat or a man to man assignment versus the opposition's passing game. Therefore, our weak outside linebacker must be quick enough to play man to man pass defense and strong enough to stop the off-tackle play to the weak side.

WEAK SIDE LINEBACKER (REGULAR POSITION) "66"

The weak side linebacker lines up in his regular position. He is coached to key the near back through the head of the tackle (Diagram 4-23).

On the snap of the ball, he should read the blocking pattern of the offensive tackle and near back or pulling inside offensive linemen. As he attacks the ball, he should focus on the triangle of the quarterback, near back and offensive tackle. This is all done on the run (Diagram 4-24).

The weak side linebacker is coached to contain the sweep to his side. If possible he should use a force-contain attack which will squeeze the play to his inside. If flow goes away, he should check for the counters,

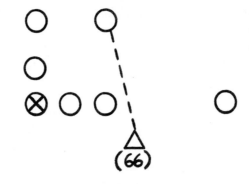

Diagram 4-23

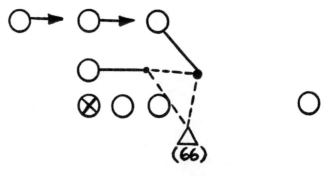

Diagram 4-24

bootlegs, etc., and then get into his correct pursuit pattern. If a sprint out pass comes his way, he is coached to attack the passer from an outside-in angle or drop back into the hook and then the curl zone. This assignment versus the sprint out pass depends upon his pre-game assigned strategy.

OUTSIDE LINEBACKER DRILLS (FORTY DEFENSE)

The three following linebacker drills, Scallop Drill (Diagram 4-25) Seven Man Hand Shiver Drill (Diagram 4-26), and the Outside Linebacker Reaction Drill (Diagram 4-27), all teach the outside linebackers to deliver a blow, get rid of the blocker (dummie), and then pursue the ball carrier.

The Pride Drill (Diagram 4-28) may be used not only for the outside linebackers but for our entire defensive football team. This is the best defensive drill in football for developing pride in the defenders' huddle, stance, alignment, reaction and pursuit angles.

Scallop Drill

Objective: Teach defender to scallop down the line reading the ball carrier, maintain proper leverage on the ball carrier, defeat the block, and make the block.

Organization: Five stand up dummies are placed in a row with five dummies opposite the stand ups lying horizontally. The blocker leads the ball carrier and the defender keys the ball carrier.

Execution: The ball carrier follows the path of the blocker and cuts up through the hole selected by the lead blocker. The defender stays on the hip of the ball carrier so he does not overrun the ball carrier. The defender scallops down the line, running over the horizontal dummies. Teach the defender to deliver a blow on the blocker, get rid of him, and then make the tackle.

Coaching Points: Drill should be used slowly without the blocker the first few times. Make sure the defender executes his shoulders parallel to the line of dummies and coach him to gather himself up into a good football hitting position just prior to attacking the blocker and ball carrier. The defender should never wait for the blocker; he should go up and meet him in the hole. The ball carrier may also cut back on the scalloping defender as illustrated in the dotted line. This cutback makes the defender scallop under control, staying parallel to the ball carrier's hip (Diagram 4-25).

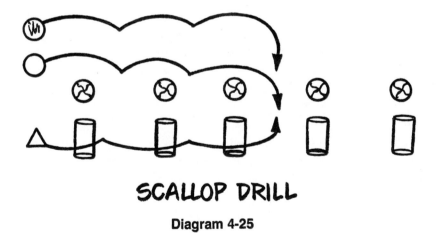

SCALLOP DRILL

Diagram 4-25

Seven Man Hand Shiver Drill

Objective: Teach hand shiver and proper foot work.

Organization: Seven man sled, hit every pad.

Execution: Defensive men line up in single file and shuffle down the line delivering a forearm shiver on each pad. Defender is taught to step up and hit sled with both arms and shuffle to next pad. The shoulder should be parallel to the sled on each hit. Good technique should be stressed rather than the speed of the defender.

Coaching Points: Quick, short, chopping, machine gun-like steps should be used by each defender. Coach must emphasize the arms of the forearm shiver should be straight with the elbows locked. If the elbows are bent, the defender will get too close to the defender's legs (Diagram 4-26).

HAND SHIVER DRILL

Diagram 4-26

Outside Linebacker's Reaction Drill

Objective: React to block and movement of ball carrier that linebacker will face in game.

Organization: Line up five dummies in center, guard, and tackle positions. Use a quarterback and a blocking offensive end versus two defensive outside linebackers.

Execution: Defensive end explodes into blocker or reacts to the direction of the ball carrier. The outside linebacker should move on movement, fight pressure, react to the potential pass, and pursue. Both linebackers should work together on sprint outs, with one in the flat or attacking the sprint out and the back side outside linebacker should drop back, cushioning for the potential throw back pass.

Coaching Points: Coach all the outside linebacker's reactions including movement, explosion, read, and reaction to the pass (Diagram 4-27).

All-Out Pursuit: The most outstanding new coaching point which has improved our pursuit tremendously has been the circle technique. The defensive coordinator points out a ten yard circle, using the ball or the ball

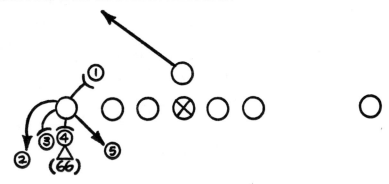

REACTION DRILL

Diagram 4-27

carrier as the radius, and it is the assignment of all our defenders to get into this circle once the whistle blows the ball dead.[3]

Our staff uses this circle technique in scrimmages and in films. During the viewing of films, we use an actual circle which we place over the projected picture reinforcing the circle pursuit technique. The players have used this circle to prove to the defensive coaches how much their pursuit has improved. In our game films we have used this coaching method of subtracting a point from the defensive player's game score if he does not make the circle.

In defensive scrimmages we have two whistles to emphasize the circle pursuit technique. The first whistle is blown when the ball is dead, no more contact; the second whistle freezes all of the defensive players. This means as soon as the defenders hear the second whistle, they must stop in their tracks and freeze so that the defensive coaches can review both their pursuit courses or channels, and make sure all of the defenders have made the ten yard pursuit circle. All of the defenders are urged to get a piece of the ball or ball carrier.

Fanatical pursuit made up from second and third effort can often make up for several defensive mistakes. In practice we also use a slow whistle drill to make sure all of our defenders pursue all the way to the ball carrier during our pursuit phase of the practice session.

---

[3]*Coaching Note:* There are, of course, a few isolated exceptions to this coaching point depending upon the backside's deep pursuit on a sweep to the opposite side of the field, or a completed pass against a man to man defense which makes it almost impossible for a backside cornerback to make the circle if his man runs an opposite sideline pass pattern.

Pride Drill: This is an excellent team pursuit drill that teaches pride in the defensive huddle, reaction, and team pursuit. It is an excellent team drill which helps to teach the entire Forty Defensive team the correct pursuit courses to head off the ball carrier.

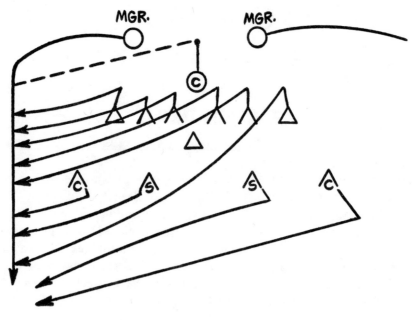

Diagram 4-28

Objective: Develops strict attention and pride in the huddle, stance, alignment, reaction, and pursuit angles.

Organization: Coach sets the ball down and defenders line up in their normal alignment. Two managers act as halfbacks who may receive the ball and sprint downfield.

Execution: Defensive team lines up in a sharp defensive open huddle. Linebacker signal caller waits until he has the complete attention of all players. Coach makes sure eyes are glued on signal caller and hands are clasped on the backs of the last row of defenders. Linebacker calls the defense and entire team breaks and lines up in unison. All of the defenders react to the movement of the ball and then make their primary charge or read steps; they then take their proper pursuit course to the ball carrier. All of the defenders must touch the ball carrier, sprint back into a class huddle and break, and line up behind the offense.

Coaching Points: If the huddle break is not perfect, the coach makes the defense realign the huddle all over again until the execution is perfect. The coach may also throw a pass; and, if the defender intercepts the ball, all of the defenders must form up a convoy group and escort him across an imaginary goal line ten yards beyond the line of scrimmage. Then the entire team must re-huddle for the team break. Three or four defensive units may run this drill in quick succession. Coaches' choice of best unit develops pride and competition (Diagram 4-28).

EVALUATING TEACHING AFTER PRACTICE DRILLS

A good coach is a good teacher. A good coach must constantly evaluate his teaching. Since we do not scrimmage for at least five practice sessions of double practice sessions, we evaluate all of our linebackers in each practice session. The defensive checklist used to evaluate the defensive linebackers in daily practice sessions is as follows:

CHECK LIST FOR EVALUATION OF LINEBACKERS IN DRILLS

	Mon.	Tues.	Wed.	Thurs.	Fri.	Sat.
1. Position and Alignment						
a. Line up and depth						
b. Mental errors—angles						
c. Physical errors—movement						
2. Key						
a. Reading						
b. Reaction						
3. Pass Reactions						
a. Pass recognition						
b. Drop course						
c. Play the ball						
4. Plug hole						
a. Correct recognition						
b. Shuffle movement						
c. Attack route						
5. Scallop						
a. Movement to ball carrier						
b. Fight pressure						
c. Correct pursuit course						
6. Tackling						
a. Approach						
b. Contact						
c. Follow through						

COACHING PROGRESSION EXPLOSION FROM A FOUR POINT STANCE

The defensive line coach must take a great deal of time to explain the teaching progression of how the defensive tackle must deliver a blow from his four point stance. We teach explosion in a form teaching progression of ten teaching phases.

First: We put the defender in a six point stance and have him explode into a two or seven man sled. From the six point stance, we fire the forearm at a target just under the offensive lineman's shoulder pads and explode off the legs, extending the bent knees at a straight angle into the defender and raising the eyes to the sky. (We mark the target on the sled's pads.) The feet should remain planted and the defender should extend himself up and into the target area and land straight on his stomach.

Second: The same method is used, but from a four point stance. We emphasize the importance of exploding from anchored feet—up, under, and through the sled's target area.

Third: Using the same method from the four point stance, we teach the defender to follow through with short choppy steps to force the defender to follow through with his explosive charge. During this third phase, we emphasize the explosive charge with the follow-up short choppy steps.

Fourth: Explode from the six point stance into a live target. Emphasize the importance of exploding the forearm into the defender's target, just under the shoulder pads.

Fifth: Explode from the four point stance into an offensive man. Emphasize the follow through of extending the knees and hips up and through the defender and lifting the eyes toward the sky.

Sixth: Explode into the offensive blocker, driving under the potential blocker and bring the feet up in short choppy steps.

Seventh: The seventh phase is to have the offensive blocker shoot for an inside or outside area on the defender. Emphasize the importance of stepping with the same foot and deliver a blow with the same arm. The defender must stay low and protect his feet.

Eighth: After delivering the blow and getting his feet going, the defender must be taught to get rid of the blocker. The opposite hand that he delivers the blow with should be used to rid the opponent. Emphasize the defender reading the head of the blocker. He should never go around the blocker's head.

Ninth: The defender should assume a good solid low football position and locate the ball. Emphasize that the defender's shoulders must be parallel to the line of scrimmage, and his feet must be under his body so he can take a lead step in any direction to cut off the ball carrier.

Tenth: Teach the defender to read and defend against the double team or the two on one block. The defender is taught to explode into the post blocker and then fight the pressure of the lead blocker. We emphasize, "meet power with power," going down on all fours if the defender must to hold his ground. We teach the defender to split the double team by submarining and by wedging his shoulder in between the two blockers. We teach the spin out only as a last resort. When the defender uses this method, he must spin as close to the lead blocker as possible. If the defender is being beaten by the double team block, we coach the defender to move back off the line slightly. This forces the blockers to go a longer way to reach the defender and also gives the defender a longer time to read the double team block.

Another teaching method we use in fighting the "perfect" double team block is to place the defender in the middle of the "perfect" double team block with the postman's head into the defender's numbers, and the drive blocker shoulder into the defender's crest of the ilium (hip). Once the blockers are fitted into the perfect block, we teach the defender (slow motion) how to fight out fo the most difficult situation. After teaching the defender the above methods of fighting out of the block, we fit him into the "perfect block" situation and blow the whistle, and let them go full speed. If a defender can fight himself out of this negative situation, he most certainly can do an outstanding job of defending against the "perfect" block situation.

These ten teaching phases help to teach the important defensive techniques of moving on movement, delivering a blow, chopping the feet, staying low in a good football position, keeping the shoulders parallel to the line of scrimmage, fighting pressure, shedding the blocker, locating the ball, and stepping in the proper direction for the correct pursuit course.

Throughout the entire football season, we drill the defensive down linemen against offensive blockers and a ball carrier. This continually exposes the defender to the multi-game-like blocking situations so that he can key, explode, and react to the many offensive blocking patterns.

COACHING DEFENSIVE DOWN LINEMEN TECHNIQUES

Line up in a four point stance with the hands parallel to each other, fingers turned slightly to the outside. The hands should be lined up directly in front of the feet. The feet should be set about shoulder width with the weight of the feet on the toes. The feet should be parallel, although we do let some of our linemen stagger the feet in a heel-toe relationship. We want the feet up under the defender so he will be able to explode out of his four point stance; therefore, the defender must bend his ankles and knees over his toes. The defender's weight should be evenly distributed over both his hands and his feet.

This defensive linemen's stance is referred to as a "bunched four point stance," which is in contrast to the elongated stance some defensive linemen use with their feet wide apart and knees straight.

The defender who lines head up on the offensive lineman must be taught to read the head of the blocker. If the blocker comes directly at the defender, the defensive man must deliver a blow on the blocker and then react to the ball carrier. To teach this head up technique, we place our defender head up on the blocker and place a ball carrier directly behind the blocker. The coach stands directly behind the defensive linemen and signals both the blocker and the ball carrier to run in a specific pattern. This helps our head up defender to hit the offensive blocker with a strong blow, get rid of the blocker, and then get ready to take on the ball carrier in a good football hitting position. Next, the coach may signal the offensive blocker to set up in a pass protection block. The defender reads pass and attacks, using his various rush the passer techniques. Once he has maneuvered past the offensive line blocker, he must next fight his way past the offensive back, protecting for the passer.

Then we progress with our defensive linemen to challenge two offensive blockers in our two on one drill. Next, our defender is ready for the three on one drill. We never move on to the next progressive drill until we are sure the defender is ready for the next step.

The defensive coaching staff must emphasize the importance of the defender to fight against the blocker's or blockers' pressure. This means if the blocker attempts to block the defender to the inside, the defender should fight against the blocker's pressure or spin out, fighting to get to the outside area.

COACHING THE DEFENSIVE LOOP TECHNIQUE

The defensive lineman is coached to take a quick short forty-five degree angle step in the direction of his outside loop, then crossover step with his inside foot, and bring the inside arm up and through the blocker's neck. When looping from a man up alignment to another man's area, the looping defender must be ready to read the blocker's head. If the blocker moves away from the looping defender, the defensive man is taught to shoot directly off the offensive man's butt. If the ball continues to go away from the defender, he should flatten out his pursuit course and pursue the ball carrier. If the man attacks the looping lineman right now, the defender is taught to drive directly through the head of the blocker, fight pressure, and then pursue the ball. One technique we use is to butt the blocker with the defender's helmet. If the offensive blocker is trying to hook the man over him, the looping lineman is coached to get a piece of the blocker as he continues his loop. If the offensive man sets up to pass block, the looping defender is coached to hit directly into the blocker and then use his normal pass rush techniques.[4]

---

[4]The defender usually attacks the blocker head up and then attempts to turn the blocker's shoulders to be able to get by the pass blocker.

Chapter 5

Split Forty Defense

TACKLES—"23"

The tackle's inside hand should be placed opposite the outside foot of the offensive guard. The top of the defensive tackle's helmet should be even to the outside shoulder of the offensive guard. The defender may be taught to use an "angled-in" or a parallel four point stance. The back should be straight, with the tail just slightly higher than the back. The head should be up so he can key the offensive guard's movement. A parallel stance is encouraged, and the tackle is taught to take his first step into the offensive guard with the inside foot (Diagram 5-1).

The "23" defender is coached to fire directly through the head and neck of the offensive guard. He is coached to gain penetration of one yard. He should take a lead step with the inside foot, and then bring his back foot up so that he gains a parallel position to the line of scrimmage. The reason he is taught to square off his shoulders is to stop the offensive trapping game. He is responsible to close off the inside trap block. If the guard fires directly into the tackle, he must fight pressure, get rid of the blocker, and attack the ball carrier. If the offensive tackle blocks down on the defensive tackle, he is coached to fight pressure, protecting himself with the outside arm, and spin off and pursue the ball carrier.

The defensive tackle is coached to key the movement of the offensive guard and not allow the offensive guard out to block the inside linebacker. If the guard pulls across the center's original position, the defender should close down quickly and take a flat pursuit course to bring the ball carrier down from behind. If the guard pulls across the tail of the tackle, the defender should fight the pressure of the tackle's block. The "23" defender is taught to spin shallow off the outside foot. The defensive tackle must stay low with his head up at all times. He must use his arms to protect his legs from the offensive cut-off blocks. One anti-trap

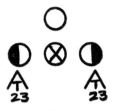

Diagram 5-1

technique is to take on the trapper with the inside shoulder, the shoulders being parallel to the line of scrimmage. This technique of using the inside shoulder and the inside arm is one of the best ways to close off the trap hole. If the defensive tackle gets out of position and penetrates too deep, he may have to reverse his body and hit the trapper with his outside shoulder. Again, this is only used as a last resort after the defender has penetrated doo deeply into the opposition's backfield.

The defensive tackle may adjust his position, when lining up on the short or split end side, by moving in closer to the offensive guard. This is accomplished by lining up the top of his helmet even with the outside eye of the offensive guard. Another adjustment is used versus a man in motion. When the linebacker yells "slide," the tackle away from the motion man assumes a parallel stance, head up on the offensive guard in a "2" alignment (if the tackle is on the split end's side).

When the offensive quarterback drops straight back into his pocket for a pass, the tackle is coached to attack the inside shoulder of the offensive guard, make an outside rush and keep in his rushing lane. Whenever the tackle rushes the passer, he should keep the blocker away from his body with his arms. Just as the passer is set to throw, the tackle is taught to get both of his arms in the air to obstruct the passer's vision and attempt to block the pass. The defensive rusher should never leave his feet until the ball is actually in the air.

INSIDE LINEBACKERS—"11"

The linebacker's head should split the center and guard gap. He should be an arm's length from the defensive tackle's heels. The defensive coach must continually check the inside linebacker's depth because these linebackers will be continually edging up closer to the line of scrimmage. It is important for the linebackers to remain in their depth to be able to read and react to the ball carrier. The linebacker's stance should consist of parallel shoulders with the outside foot dropped back slightly in a parallel toe-instep relationship. These defenders should be in a two point, semi-crotched stance with the arms hanging freely in front of the legs (Diagram 5-2).

Diagram 5-2

The linebacker should key the quarterback's first step and then pick up the action of the near back. The linebacker is then coached to play the near hole responsibility up to the off tackle hole. The linebacker should scallop down the line, gaining ground slightly until he can meet the ball carrier head on with his shoulders parallel to the goal line. He must never be blocked by the center or the offensive guard. If the tackle blocks down on the defensive tackle, the inside linebacker should slide to the outside and look for the potential block by the offensive tight end. The linebacker should stay on the hip of the ball carrier, being careful never to over run the ball carrier. If the action of the backs goes away from the linebacker, he should shuffle over to head up on the center, keeping his depth with his shoulders parallel to the line of scrimmage. The linebacker should look for any inside plays, then check for counters or traps; then, pursue the ball if it goes away from his immediate area of responsibility. If the action pass comes at the linebacker, he should attack through his area of responsibility or drop back to his hook zone area, depending upon the defensive stunt or defensive pass coverage call. When play action pass develops away from the inside linebacker, he must get depth and set a course for the deep middle one-third zone, or play the defensive pass coverage previously called in the defensive huddle. If the quarterback drops straight backward in a pocket pass, the linebacker should drop back quickly in his prescribed hook zone area.

The inside linebacker to the split end's side must adjust his "11" alignment if the offensive formation is loaded or strong to his side. If this happens, the inside linebacker to the loaded side should stack behind the defensive tackle. From his position he must be able to go back to stop the inside play or quickly scallop over to the off tackle play. The other Split Forty inside linebacker should line up head on the center. This gives the middle a regular 40 look. The "00" defensive linebacker is responsible for the quick middle trap and the offensive inside counters. Whenever a man goes in motion, the linebackers slide over toward the direction of the motion. This usually gives the defense a regular 40 look over the middle, with an extra linebacker in the direction of the motion man. The linebackers also slide over in the direction of strong or loaded offensive attack. This formation usually places two backs to the same side (Diagram 5-3).

Diagram 5-3

ENDS "8" (OR "6" TO THE SPLIT END SIDE)

The Split 40 defensive end lines up in his "8" position with his inside hand one yard outside of the offensive end. The defender is angled in toward the near back. The stance is an optional three or four point stance with the inside leg back and the inside hand down (in the three point stance, Diagram 5-4).

The defender moves on the offensive blocker's movement and delivers a blow and attacks through the blocker's head. The inside foot is forward; therefore, he delivers a blow stepping with the inside foot and

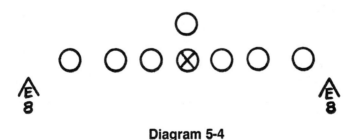

Diagram 5-4

delivering a forearm blow, if the blocker attempts to block high. If the blocker attempts to scramble block the defensive end, he should use his arms to keep the blocker away from his legs. The defender must realize he must contain all of the opposition's runs.

Key the halfback through the end's head. If the halfback drives directly at the end, he should meet the blocker nose on nose and smash him with the inside arm. If the halfback goes to the end's outside, force the play and read on the move. If the halfback goes inside of the end, the defender is coached to close down through the blocker's outside shoulder. He should neutralize the offensive end's block if he turns out on the defensive end. The defender must then hold up until he is sure the play is going to his inside. He must attack the ball carrier from an inside-outside angle.

The "6" alignment to the split end or short side places the end with the same responsibilities as the regular "8" alignment and technique. The difference is that when the defensive end is on the split end's side, he must break down in a good football position after only two steps with the outside foot back. Our defensive staff refers to this as "hiding the outside leg." After the defender shuffles to this position, he should concentrate on his key—the near back. If run shows, he should close the inside hole off and the "6" defender does not have as much contain responsibility as the defensive end has to the tight end's side.

To the split end's side the defensive end may have contain help from the outside linebacker. If pass shows, the defender must use his contain rush on most passes. If the passer attempts to scramble, the end should realize that the outside linebacker may be able to help him on a wide scramble, but not on a run to the inside.

The defensive end in the Split 40 Defense plays the following run and pass actions in the following ways:

1. Power Sweep, Pro Sweep or Sprint Out To—Take the ball (Diagram 5-5).
2. Power Sweep, Pro Sweep, or any action away—Look for the waggle, counter, or bootleg, and if none of these show, pursue straight for the ball (Diagram 5-6).
3. Option Action To—Play cat and mouse with the quarterback. Keep your eyes on him; make him commit himself. Keep shoulders parallel to the line of scrimmage and try to make the quarterback string out option. If he keeps the ball and turns up field, attack him (Diagram 5-7).
4. Inside Belly To—Play the ball (Diagram 5-8).

5. Outside Belly Action To—Play the quarterback (Diagram 5-9).
6. Teen Action To—Take the ball (Diagram 5-10).
7. Straight Drop Back Pocket Pass—Rush from the outside-in angle. Must keep outside leverage on passer. Rush passer with arms up and tackle the passer from the top down (Diagram 5-11).

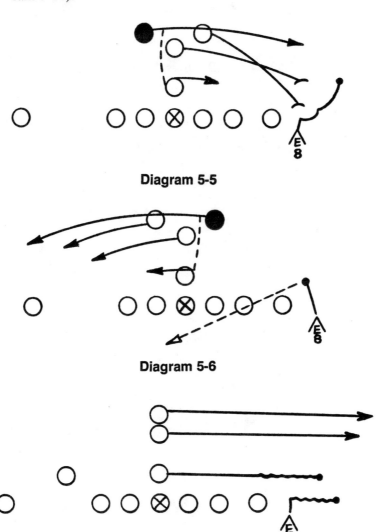

Diagram 5-5

Diagram 5-6

Diagram 5-7

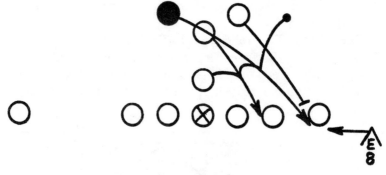

Diagram 5-8

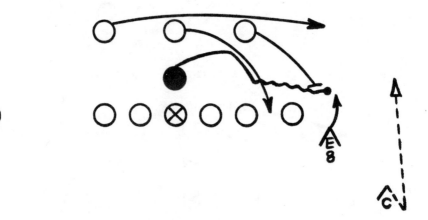

Diagram 5-9

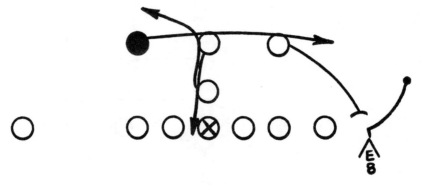

Diagram 5-10

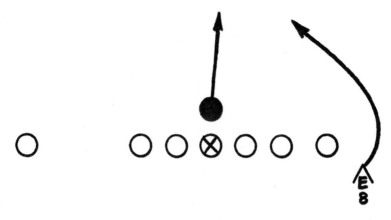

Diagram 5-11

OUTSIDE LINEBACKER—"65" OR "66"

The outside linebacker should line up splitting the offensive end's inside foot one yard off the line of scrimmage. He should use a two point stance with his inside leg forward. He should keep his shoulders parallel to the line of scrimmage, and he must protect his inside leg from a reach block by the offensive tackle or a scramble block by the offensive end (Diagram 5-12).

Key the offensive end if in the "65" technique first; then, check the offensive tackle. If stacked "66" to the split end's side, key the tackle or near back. If flow goes away, the linebacker should chug the receiver, check for the reverse or bootleg action, then drop back into his predetermined defensive pass coverage assignment.

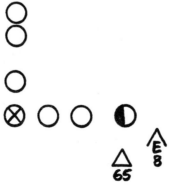

Diagram 5-12

The defensive outside linebacker's reaction depends upon the offensive formation. If two receivers split to the defender's outside and the run comes to the defender, he should come up and attack the run from an outside-in angle. If pass shows, he should play the predetermined pass coverage call. If in doubt, the outside linebacker should hold until he is sure what the offensive maneuver is. When there are two backs and an end to the linebacker's side, he should move out on the first back, outside of the end, and play two to three yards deep head-up on the first wide back. If a straight drop back pocket pass shows, the linebacker must sprint back to his defensive flat zone area. When one man is removed from the backfield to the outside linebacker's side or one man is split to his side, he should read and play the off tackle hole first. If he is not sure it is a run or pass action to his side, he should hold until he is sure of the play.

ADJUSTMENTS FOR END AND OUTSIDE LINEBACKERS

These are the Split 40 defensive adjustments used by the defensive ends and outside linebackers against strong, wing, split end, slot and flanker formations. These linebacker and end adjustments may be predetermined prior to the game, called in the defensive huddle, called on the spot as soon as the offense sets up their formation, or a combination of these three plans.

1. Against a split end, the defensive end and linebacker may stack with the linebacker reading the offensive tackle's block. For example, if the tackle shows pass, the linebacker would drop back into his flat zone (Diagram 5-13).

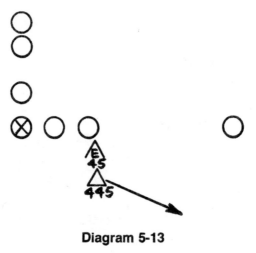

Diagram 5-13

2. The outside linebacker may also be called into a double cover position where he would line up just to the inside of the wide receiver. When double coverage is used by the outside linebacker, the other linebackers slide over to compensate for the outside linebacker's departure (Diagram 5-14). The other linebackers may also remain in their normal Split 40 alignments (Diagram 5-15).

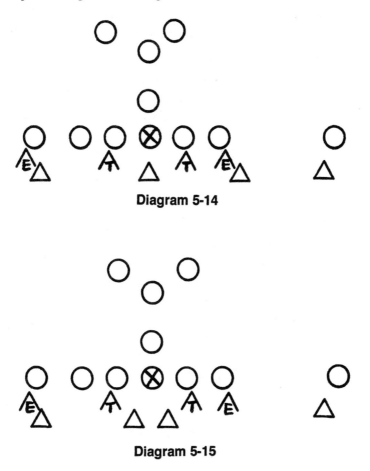

Diagram 5-14

Diagram 5-15

3. When the defensive end and outside linebacker adjust to a wingback, the linebacker moves head up on the defensive end in a "6" position, with a one- to two-yard split by the wingback (Diagram 5-16). The defensive end drives into the wingback's outside shoulder.

4. If the wingback splits out to three yards, the linebacker remains in his regular "6" alignment, but now the defensive end drives into the nose of the wingback instead of over his outside shoulder as in Diagram 5-17.

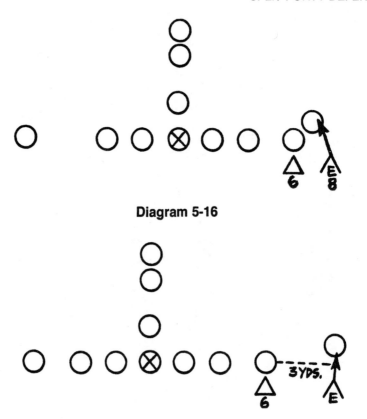

Diagram 5-16

Diagram 5-17

5. When the wingback flanks out four or more yards, the defensive linebacker plays his normal ''6'' technique and the defensive end moves into his normal ''8'' technique, as long as he can beat the flanker across the line. At times the defensive end is given an alternative of lining head up on the flanked wingback at four yards, and then jumping to his regular ''8'' alignment just prior to the snap of the ball (Diagram 5-18).

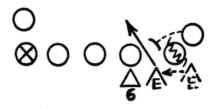

Diagram 5-18

6. Against a nasty (three to four yards) split by the offensive end, the defensive end and linebacker switch their positions, which puts the end on the inside, in a "5" alignment, and the linebacker plays head up on the offensive end (Diagram 5-19).

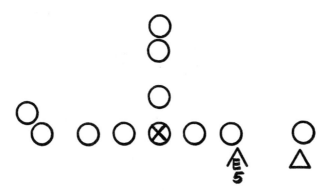

Diagram 5-19

7. When facing a tight slot, the two outside defenders can play normally or exchange their positions as in Diagram 5-20. Against the slot, the defensive end attacks through the slot man's head and the linebacker plays head up on the offensive end (Diagram 5-20).

Diagram 5-20

The normal alignment and immediate responsibilities of the entire team defense are in Diagram 5-21. The inside split linebackers ("11") are responsible for the one gap, the defensive tackles ("23") check the three gap, the outside linebackers ("65" or "66") are assigned the five gap area, and the defensive ends ("8") are assigned outside defensive containment (Diagram 5-21).

When facing a Pro "I" formation with two wide receivers to each side and no running backs in the regular halfback running or set positions, the outside linebackers can be lined up in one of four positions. These positions include a normal, stacked, walk-away, or double cover position (Diagram 5-22).

If the eight man front faces a twin set or two wide receivers to one side, the linebacker to that side must use his rule of thumb alignment. This means he must never be outflanked by two wide receivers; therefore, he is assigned to line up on the inside receiver and react from there (Diagram 5-23).

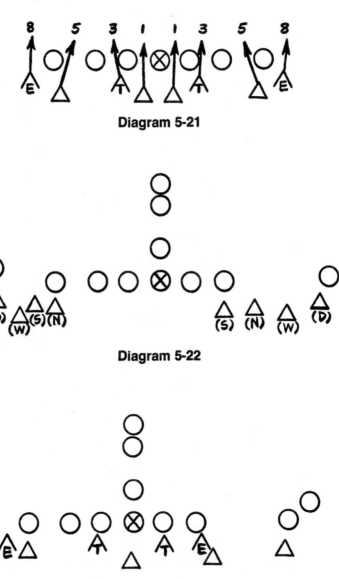

Diagram 5-21

Diagram 5-22

Diagram 5-23

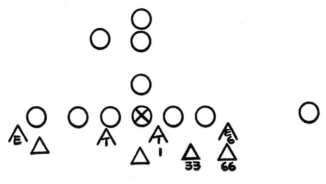

Diagram 5-24

One more adjustment that may be used to the split end's side is to offset the defensive tackle. The offset tackle now is responsible to shoot through the one gap on all fours and key the quarterback's movement. The inside linebacker closest to the split end moves over and lines up ("33" alignment) off the line between the short side guard and tackle gap. The end lines up in his normal "6" technique with the outside linebacker stacked behind him (Diagram 5-24).

Chapter 6

Split Forty Adjustments
and Stunts

SPLIT 40 DEFENSE 1-2-3 BLITZES

The Split 40 Defense features the same 1-2-3 blitzes as featured in the normal 40 Defense. We can move very quickly from the 40 Defense to the Split 40 Defense by just sliding over the weakside linebacker to an inside weak linebacker, moving the "00" middle man to "11," and moving the weak safetyman up into the outside weak linebacker's regular "66" position (Diagram 6-1).

The basic method of shifting from the 40 to Split 40 Defense is to move a rover man from an "8" alignment (walk-away), 44 alignment (eagle), or an inside safety alignment from a four deep alignment (Diagram 6-2).

If the defensive signal caller calls a Split 41, the one linebacker who is in a "66" alignment fires through the same "3" gap as he did in the 40 Defense. Both the right end and right tackle have their same assignments as the "1" call from the 40 Defense (Diagram 6-3).

The Split 41 Blitz is not used as much as the normal 41 Blitz because the inside split linebacker (11) to the outside linebacker's side usually scrapes off into this one area. The scrape off usually takes place when offensive flow moves in the direction of the linebacker. Therefore, the one blitz is usually called by the signal caller whenever a straight drop back or pull up pass is anticipated.

When Split 42 is called, the "2" linebacker fires through the "3" gap to the tight end's side similar to the normal 42 call. The tackle to the tight end's side lines head up on the offensive right guard so he can shoot into the "1" gap (Diagram 6-4).

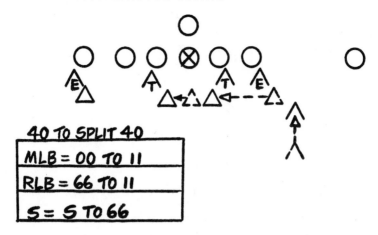

40 TO SPLIT 40
MLB = 00 TO 11
RLB = 66 TO 11
S = S TO 66

SHIFT FROM 40 TO SP. 40 DEFENSE

Diagram 6-1

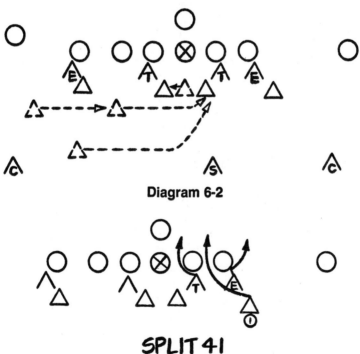

Diagram 6-2

SPLIT 41

Diagram 6-3

SPLIT 42

Diagram 6-4

Split 43 call sends the three linebacker through the "5" gap and the defensive left end steps to his outside so that he can contain any wide maneuver to his side (Diagram 6-5).

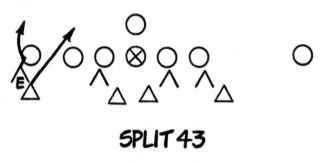

SPLIT 43

Diagram 6-5

When the defensive signal caller calls for a Split 40 All, all (1-2-3) three of the linebackers blitz into their prescribed areas. A man to man defensive secondary call usually accompanies the triple blitz call. This means that the right defensive cornerback picks up the split end to his side, the inside split linebacker to the split side (11) takes the next inside receiver (opponent's left halfback), the strong safetyman is matched up with the tight end, and the left defensive halfback plays the wide receiver man to man (Diagram 6-6).

The right inside split linebacker (versus two tight ends) or the inside split linebacker to the split end's side is the rover defender. If the signal caller calls for a Monster Alignment versus a Pro Offensive Set, this rover defender would line up in a monster position to the flanker back's side (Diagram 6-7). This would then force the defensive front into a seven man look as in Diagram 6-8 or Diagram 6-9.

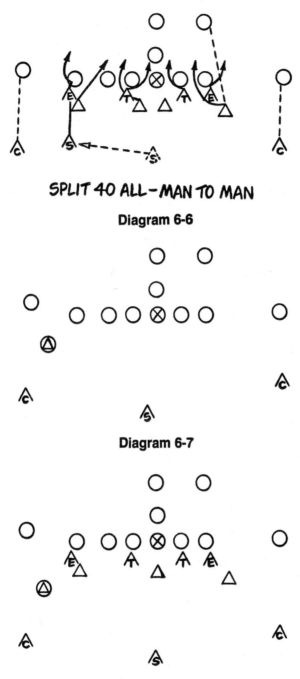

SPLIT 40 ALL-MAN TO MAN

Diagram 6-6

Diagram 6-7

Diagram 6-8

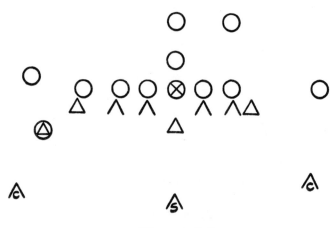

Diagram 6-9

SPLIT FORTY MIDDLE STUNTS

Along with the regular one, two, three stunts, we use a group of middle stunts which involve only the four interior defenders (two tackles and two inside linebackers). These middle unit stunts consist of:

Split 40 In
Split 40 Out
Split 40 In-Out
Split 40 Out-In
Split 40 Twist (Left inside linebacker goes first)
Split 40 Fire (Backside linebacker)
Split 40 Flash
Tackles Read

Split 40 In (Diagram 6-10): The "In" indicates the tackles stunt through the "1" gaps, while the linebackers are coached to blitz through the "3" gaps. This stunt is an excellent middle unit maneuver against an offense who favors a straight drop-back passing attack. The Split 40 In stunt usually frees at least one defender, as the unit stunt features a 4 to 3 defensive-offensive ratio. The defensive tackles are coached to use more of a "2" or head up alignment so they can be sure to loop into their "1" gaps respectively. The split inside linebackers loop to the "3" gaps and are taught to reach their points (even with the original position of the offensive guards' and tackles' feet), with their shoulders parallel to the line of scrimmage and in a good football position. The linebackers must

Diagram 6-10

be ready to pursue the ball carrier on a flat course to the right or the left. The defensive tackles are now responsible for the quarterback sneak and the middle draw play.

Split 40 Out (Diagram 6-11): The middle unit now exchanges their stunts with the linebackers blitzing straight through the "1" gaps and the

Diagram 6-11

tackles looping through the "3" gaps. The defensive assignments are also exchanged with the defensive tackles responsible for the quarterback sneak and inside draw plays. This middle stunt is also excellent against the straight drop back pass and is also most successful in breaking up the timing versus the triple option maneuver. The inside linebacker to the isde of the play is often on top of the quarterback so quickly that he hits the quarterback, just as he is about to hand or fake the ball off to the first man on the triple option. This blitz often causes a fumble or creates confusion and poor timing on the triple option. This is also a fine maneuver versus any quick offensive play up the middle, particularly versus the quick trap play. The blitzing linebacker is often on top of the ball carrier just as he is about ready to take the hand-off.

The continual threat of the Split 40 Out stunt also minimizes the interior offensive linemen's offensive line split, which cuts down upon the offensive interior attacking consistency.

Split 40 In-Out (Diagram 6-12): The In-Out call changes up the stunt between the left and right defensive tackles and linebackers. The

Diagram 6-12

first word signifies the left side of the middle unit, and the second word represents the right side of the middle unit. The offensive attack and field position should determine when and which way to call this stunt. As the left linebacker begins to move toward his ''3'' gap destination, he should keep his eye on the ball. Once he gets the direction from the ball key, he reads the blocks of the guard and tackle to his side. If the ball goes away and the guard blocks toward the center, the left linebacker's loop is shortened, and he should begin to take a flat angle for the ball as soon as possible (Diagram 6-13).

Diagram 6-13

Split 40 Out-In (Diagram 6-14): The Out calls for the left tackle to loop out into the ''3'' gap, while the In signals the right tackle to loop inside, into the ''1'' gap. As soon as the left linebacker blitzes into the ''1'' gap and the right linebacker fires into the ''3'' gap, they are coached

Diagram 6-14

to get their hands high in the air as soon as the passer attempts to throw. If a run develops, the charging linemen are taught to take intelligent pursuit courses, never following the same color jersey. The Split 40 In, Out, In-Out, and Out-In calls keep the offensive blockers honest and minimize their fire-out blocking techniques. The reasons the blockers must hold back on their firing out technique is that the offensive blocker must hold up and determine if his man will fire on, inside, or outside. If his man goes away, many offensive attacks teach the blocker to hold and pick up another defender shooting into his area. This type of zone block makes the blocker hold just long enough to give the defensive linemen a definite stunting advantage. If the offensive line uses definite man for man blocking rules, the defensive stunts will open up large holes for the stunting defenders to shoot through.

Split 40 Twist (Diagram 6-15): This defensive stunt helps to confuse the offensive center and guards particularly. The left linebacker is the

Diagram 6-15

defender who fires across into the "1" gap first, and the right side linebacker is assigned to delay and then twist or cross over to the left side defensive "1" gap. This slight delay usually allows the right linebacker a clean shot into the opponent's backfield.

Both of the defensive tackles are still assigned to loop out into the "3" gaps and then pursue the ball carrier. The defensive left tackle must be coached to realize that the right linebacker will be a delayed blitzer;

therefore, he must cut down the angle of his loop so that he can react to a quick dive to his inside "1" gap area. The Twist stunt is most advantageous against an anticipated drop back or sprint out pass. This stunt is also a fine call against the anticipated inside belly play and all quick inside dive plays.

Split 40 Fire (Diagram 6-16): The Split 40 Fire stunt assigns the backside linebacker to shoot into an opening area between the outside

Diagram 6-16

shoulder of the offensive guard. The linebacker who is away from offensive flow is taught to blitz, while the frontside linebacker to the flow side is coached to use his normal scrape off maneuver. Once the backside linebacker has blitzed, he is coached to locate the ball and take his proper pursuit course to attack the ball. This blitz from the backside often causes a fumble because the defender makes his tackle from the ball carrier's blindside. If a blocker attempts to reach block the blitzing linebacker, the defender should go through the head of the blocker rather than go around the blocker.

The defensive tackles are coached to read their offensive guards' blocks. We do not want the tackles to loop into the "3" gaps on the snap of the ball because this would leave too much area, from offensive guard to guard, for the backside linebacker to defend.

If the quarterback does not move in a right or left direction but rather drops straight back into a drop back pass action area, there is no designated backside linebacker; therefore, both of the linebackers are coached to revert to their regular assignments and drop back into their respective hook zones (Diagram 6-17).

Split 40 Flash (Diagram 6-18): This call fires the two inside linebackers straight through the "1" gaps just like the Split 40 Out call. The difference in the Flash call is that the defensive tackles are assigned to read rather than loop out in the "3" gaps. The reason we have the

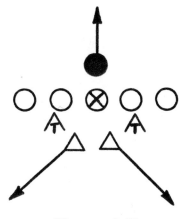

Diagram 6-17

Diagram 6-18

Flash call is just to blitz our two inside split linebackers and have the other six members of the eight man front play their regular keying on reading defense. This is a quick, surprising maneuver to put quick pressure on the quarterback.

ADDITIONAL SPLIT FORTY ADJUSTMENTS

We also adjust the Split Forty Defense in the following manner:

Forty Kill Defense (Diagram 6-19): The 40 Kill Defense gives our defense a unique look to the offensive unit. The 40 Kill features a defender in a head up position on the offensive center, "0" technique, giving the defense an odd look. The middle linebacker is stacked directly behind the nose man ("00" technique). The great advantage for the middle linebacker is that he is protected from the offensive center's quick block. It also causes a blocking unit trouble if they try to number the defensive

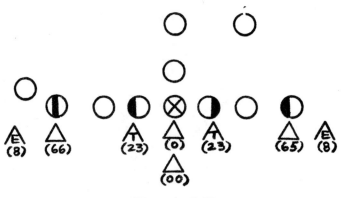

Diagram 6-19

team using the number blocking rules because the middle linebacker is usually free to roam.

This 40 Kill alignment gives the defense an excellent pattern to blitz into the offensive backfield against a powerful inside offensive running attack. It is also a strong defense to rush the passer from because it places four defenders on only three blockers, when a middle blitz is called assigning the middle linebacker to fire in on an anticipated pass play. Using this change-up forty alignment often springs one of the defenders free to attack the passer, before he has the chance to set up for his pass.

The Forty Kill Defense is also a fine defensive call against the short yardage defense; since all of the offensive linemen are covered by a defender, the middle linebacker is free to make the tackles from sideline to sideline.

Tackles:

Alignment: Line up in a "23" technique splitting the outside leg of the offensive guard with the middle of the body.

Coaching Points: Drive through the outside shoulder of the offensive guard. If the guard blocks out, fight the blocker's pressure. If the guard blocks down, close off to the inside following the path of the guard and locate the ball.

Down Nose Backer:

Alignment: Line up nose on the offensive center in a four point stance ("0" technique).

Coaching Points: Fight pressure of the offensive center's block. If blitz is called, be ready to shoot the "1" gap. Technique depends upon the middle linebacker's call.

Middle Linebacker:

Alignment: Line up directly behind the nose man in a "00" technique. Use regular up stance.

Coaching Points: React to the ball. If blitz is called, linebacker will be responsible for either "1" gap (Diagram 6-19).[1]

Forty Smash (Diagram 6-20): The Forty Smash Defense is another slight variation from the normal Split Forty Defense. This adjustment is a

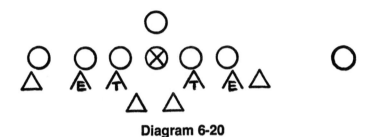

Diagram 6-20

combination of the Split Forty and Pro Forty Defenses (Diagram 6-20). The middle four unit lines up similar to the normal Split Forty Defense (tackles and split linebackers), while the defensive outside linebackers knock down the defensive ends to their normal Pro 45 techniques. The defensive linebackers then assume their "67" alignments and acquire their containment assignments. The "67" and "45" defenders use the same techniques and assignments as the Pro Forty Defense and the interior middle four use the same normal alignments, techniques and assignments as used in the Split Forty Defense. The exact same middle stunts can be used as illustrated in the Split Forty Middle Stunts (Diagrams 6-10, 11, 12, 13, 14, 15, 16, 17, 18).

SPLIT FORTY STRATEGIC ADJUSTMENTS AND STUNTS

In organizing our Split Forty Defense against each opponent, we consider four alternatives:

1. Defend against their favorite formations.

---

[1]*Coaching Note:* Outside linebackers and ends use the same alignments and techniques as the regular Split Forty Defense.

2. Take advantage of the offensive blocking patterns.

3. Stop their bread and butter offensive plays.

4. Attack their best ball carrier.

(1) *Defend against their favorite formations*—In defending against an opponent's formation we first determine, through scouting reports and film breakdowns, what the opposition likes to do from a specific formation. If the offensive formation overshifts the offense to run to the strong side, we will also overshift our normally balanced Split Forty Defense to meet power with power (Diagram 6-21). We simply move one of our

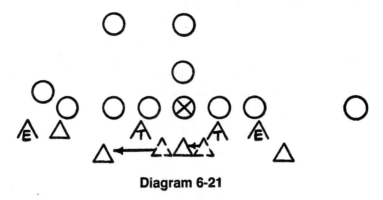

Diagram 6-21

inside linebackers to the strength of the formation (Diagram 6-21). Another way is to slide our defensive line over to the strong side of the opponent's formation (Diagram 6-22). In Diagram 6-22 we move the defensive tackle to the outside shoulder of the strong side offensive tackle

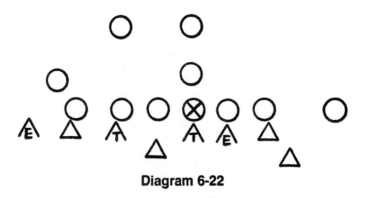

Diagram 6-22

and move over the other defenders (weak tackle, end, and linebackers) one man toward the strong side.

If we face a Power "I" formation which likes to attack the middle, we will line up in our normal Split Forty Defense and occasionally give the opponent a "seven diamond look" (Diagram 6-23). This means we just adjust the position of one of our inside linebackers to a nose position head up on the offensive center, and stack the other inside linebacker (B) making the middle of our defense a stacked odd defense (Diagram 6-23). (See Forty Kill—Diagram 6-19.)

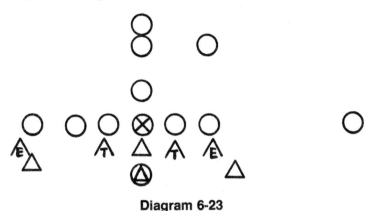

Diagram 6-23

Against a pro passing type of offense, we often align our defense in several ways. Against a definite passing threat on a third and long situation when the defense must defend against two outstanding wide offensive receivers, the defense would call a double cover call. This places double coverage on the two wide receivers and also maintains the normal three deep secondary defense (Diagram 6-24).

When we need a four deep secondary defense, we move our rover linebacker (B) away from the line of scrimmage and move him into the strong side safety position. In definite passing situations, we may substitute a deep defensive secondary defender for our rover back in this key strong safety position or play the rover linebacker in the strong safety position (B). The interior defense now takes on a normal forty defensive look (Diagram 6-25).

Against a third and short yardage situation, we may shift our rover linebacker into a normal monster position. This places our defense in a Forty Pro look with the monster or rover linebacker just outside of the tight end's position. The defense now remains in their normal three deep alignment (Diagram 6-26).

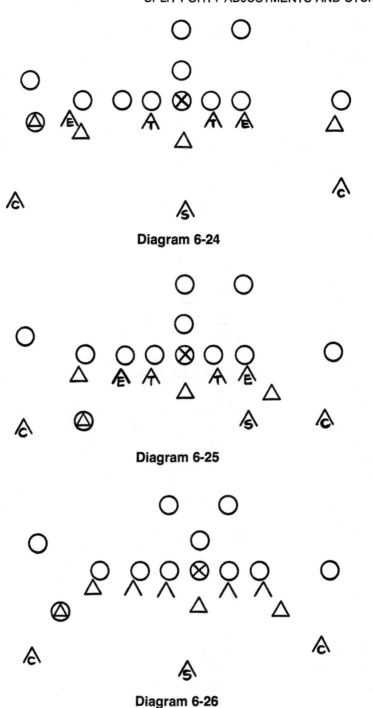

Diagram 6-24

Diagram 6-25

Diagram 6-26

(2) *Take advantage of offensive blocking patterns*—For a change of pace against certain blocking patterns, we will jump or game into different defensive looks just prior to the snap of the ball, to confuse the offensive linemen at the point of attack. Another method we employ is to call particular stunts or blitzes against certain opponents, depending upon their favorite line blocking patterns. Against a fold or step around blocking pattern, we use one of two techniques. If the opponent is trying to fold block by blocking the offensive tackle down on the defensive tackle and stepping the offensive guard around to block the inside linebacker, we emphasize the scrape or wipe off technique. This technique features the inside split forty linebacker scraping as close to the tackle as possible and then squaring his shoulders off as soon as he attacks the line of scrimmage. Using this quick upfield attacking movement usually beats the offensive guard to the punch and enables the scrape off linebacker an open shot into the open gap area (Diagram 6-27).

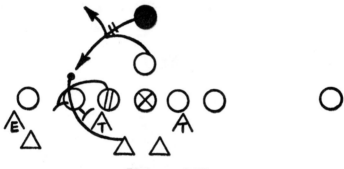

Diagram 6-27

The Out Call is another stunt where the defensive tackle steps out into the offensive tackle's down or drive block and the inside linebacker shoots into the gap between the guard and center. As the offensive guard begins his fold technique, the inside linebacker takes on a more intelligent angle (through the wider opening once movement is made by the guard) to cut off the ball carrier (Diagram 6-28). (See Split Forty In, Diagram 6-10, and Split Forty Out, Diagram 6-11.)

If the opponent uses a great deal of reach blocking (scrambling to the play side to cut off the defenders by getting the head in front of the opposition and then scrambling on all fours), we employ our predetermined fire technique by the backside inside linebacker. This means the frontside or playside offensive guard may try to cut off the defensive tackle and the center may attempt to reach block on the playside inside

Diagram 6-28

linebacker. But before the backside guard can cut off the backside linebacker, the defender fires through the large gap created by the reach blocking offensive center, (Diagram 6-29). If the firing backside linebacker is unable to make the blitz because he may get tangled up, he then bounces to the outside and scallops down the line of scrimmage to pursue the ball carrier. (See Split 40 Fire, Diagram 6-29.)

Diagram 6-29

(3) *Stop their bread and butter plays*—This fire technique is also an excellent blitz against a trapping offensive attack who likes to block back with the offensive center on the defensive tackle. This backside block helps to open up the hole for the backside linebacker to fire through and break up the trap play before it gets under way (Diagram 6-30).

Another solid call versus the trap play is a combination of an "In" to one side and an "Out" blitz by the two inside linebackers and defensive tackles. This puts four defenders stunting on three interior offensive blockers. This call helps to confuse the moving trapper as well as his

Diagram 6-30

other blocking teammates at the point of the attack (Diagram 6-31). All of these defenders are coached to shoot straight through the line and then come under control. If the defender fires through the gap and gets out of control, he is coached to drop to all fours and scramble until he comes under control. (See Split 40 In-Out, Diagram 6-12).

Diagram 6-31

The Twist stunt is the other inside blitz that helps to cause chaos among the interior offensive blockers on all trap calls. The Twist signifies that the two split linebackers cross into each other's respective guard-center gaps. While the two inside Split 40 linebackers execute their cross techniques, the two tackles loop into the guard-tackle gap (Diagram 6-32). (See Split 40 Twist, Diagram 6-15.)

On short yardage plays, when we expect the opponent to attack the

Diagram 6-32

middle of the offensive line, we will often line up in our "seven diamond look" and fire the two stacked odd defenders as the defensive tackles read the block of the offensive guards (Diagram 6-33).

Diagram 6-33

Another method to attack the offensive middle point of the attack is to offset the two defensive tackles into the gaps and coach them to fire into their respective gaps. The defensive linebackers then are taught to stack behind these two defenders and read the quarterback. The two linebackers then loop toward the point of attack. This gap alignment often takes the offensive linemen by surprise (especially when the defense jumps into this defense at the last moment just prior to the snap of the ball, Diagram 6-34). Scrapping techniques, ins, outs, and fire blitzes that have been previously diagrammed are also fine stunts to use against a powerful middle offensive attack.

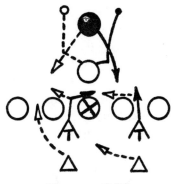

Diagram 6-34

If an opponent features an off-tackle attack to the strong side, the defensive signal caller may call for an overshifted defense and use a stunt between the outside and the overshifted inside linebacker. This stunt focuses upon the strong side linebacker blitzing into the "5" gaps (between the tight end and tackle) with the overshifted inside linebacker blitzing outside to the off-tackle area (Diagram 6-35). This stunt is also

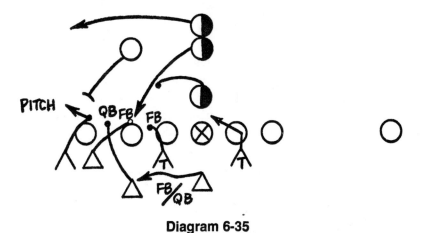

Diagram 6-35

strong against the outside belly option play where the defense can place two men on the fullback (strong side linebacker and strong side tackle), with the blitzing inside linebacker picking up the quarterback and the defensive end assigned to the pitchman[2] (Diagram 6-35). When we ex-

[2]*Coaching Note:* We use the alternative defensive maneuver versus the off-tackle belly because it is imperative to ready all defenders for a second and third alternative method against all basic plays.

pect an off-tackle drive to the strong side, we may overshift one of our inside linebackers, but this time we would put him down in a four point stance and move the offensive tackle to the outside shoulder of the offensive tackle. This gives our defense a different look with two down defensive linemen covering the strong side offensive guard and tackle. Once in this alignment, we can stunt into the off-tackle hole by driving the defensive tackle out into the tackle-end gap and bring the strong linebacker back under the guard-tackle gap (Diagram 6-36).

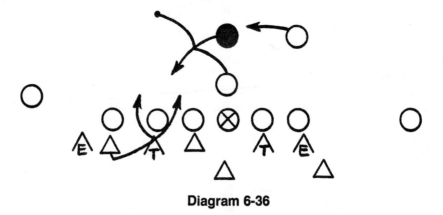

Diagram 6-36

From our normal alignment, we also attack the off-tackle power play by blitzing both the strong side linebacker and the play side inside linebacker into the off-tackle area. The outside linebacker attacks on an outside-in angle, while the inside linebacker attacks the off-tackle power play from an inside-out angle (Diagram 6-37).

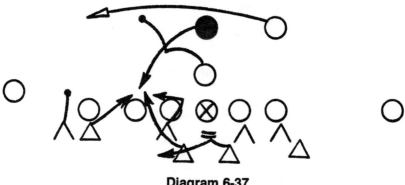

Diagram 6-37

(4) *Attacking their best ball carrier on the sweep*—Against the power or the tear sweep, we want to get as much defensive penetration as possible. We believe if our defensive end can penetrate two yards or more, we can take away the power sweep. Thus if we expect a power sweep to the short side, we will make a predetermined "Crash Call." This call is predicated upon the opponent's flow to the short side. If flow comes, we veer the tackle through the outside shoulder of the short side guard and veer the defensive end in the same manner through the outside shoulder of the offensive tackle. The weakside linebacker moves up on the line of scrimmage, just prior to the snap by the center, and veers into the flowing action. The inside Split Forty linebacker closest to the weak side uses a wide scrape-off move, heading for the outside hip of the forcing weak-side linebacker (Diagram 6-38). This crashing action by the

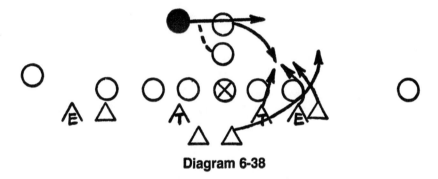

Diagram 6-38

weak-side defenders often results in a considerable loss for the power sweeping offensive attack. If we exepct a sweep to the strong side of the opponent's offensive formation, we may call a guard-tackle stack to the strong side, and then have our tackle penetrate on all fours as deep as possible and scrape the stacked linebacker off into the tackle-end gap. As soon as the stacked linebacker reaches the gap, he must make himself as small as possible to wedge freely through the gap. Once he has made penetration, he is coached to square off his shoulders, locate the ball, and take his proper pursuit course to cut off the ball carrier. The defensive end is taught to angle into the flow, keeping the lead blocker on his outside shoulder. We want the penetrating end to get depth and take on the lead blocker by exploding an inside forearm into the blocker's numbers. The strong-side linebacker is coached to chug the end, to keep this blocker off our scrapping linebacker, who is blitzing into the tackle-end gap. Then the outside linebacker is taught to hold for a split second and then loop to the outside of the veering defensive end so that the power sweep will not break containment (Diagram 6-39).[3]

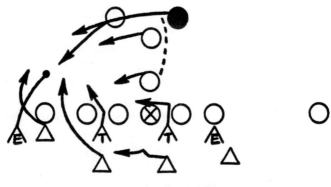

Diagram 6-39

Another method of attacking the strongside power sweep is to jump to an overshifted defense with the strong inside Split Forty linebacker lining up over the strongside guard in a down four point alignment. The defensive tackle moves out to the outside shoulder of the strongside offensive tackle (45) and reacts to the offensive tackle's block similar to an Oklahoma defensive tackle. If the offense employs a Wing-T Offense, the defensive end plays head up on the wing man with the strongside linebacker playing the outside shoulder of the offensive end (67). These two defenders have the option of exchanging positions, depending upon the defensive strategy. On the snap of the ball, all of the defenders loop to the strong side with the exception of the weakside linebacker who holds, checking for some counter action back to the weak side. The loop technique is executed by taking a short lead step to the strong side on a forty-five degree angle, always working up field. The defender must be ready to meet a blocker with the strongside forearm, but keeping the weakside forearm ready if the opponent attempts to use a cut-off block by scrambling on all fours and attempting to cut off the defensive loop by getting the blocker's head in front of the looping defender (Diagram 6-40).

Split Forty Defense Versus the Sprint Out Option—When we attack the sprint out option with the frontside halfback diving to the split

---

[3]*Coaching Note:* The strongside defensive linebacker holds for a split second until he is sure the offensive end does not use a turn-out block on the defensive end. If this happens, coupled with the strongside linebacker's outside loop, the strongside off-tackle hole would open up like a funnel.

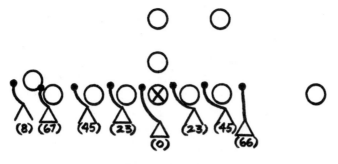

Diagram 6-40

end side, the stack defensive end and the outside linebacker are given a "You/Me" option call. This means the end and the outside linebacker may exchange responsibilities on options to the split end side. If the outside linebacker calls "you," this means the defensive end has the dive man assignment. If he yells "me," this means that he will tackle the dive man. The defender who is assigned to the dive man must always tackle this offensive back. He is never assigned the option of guessing because this may allow the dive man to break away for a long gainer, in the event the quarterback gives the ball to the dive man. If there is any mixup over the oral call or the assignment, both outside defenders must realize that the "you" call is always on, unless the linebacker makes a "me" call (Diagram 6-41).

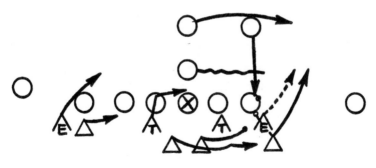

Diagram 6-41

This means in Diagram 6-41 that one of the two outside defenders is responsible for the pitchman, while the other outside defender has the dive man. The inside frontside linebacker is responsible for the quarterback if he keeps the ball, while the backside inside Split 40 linebacker checks the (1) dive, (2) quarterback keeper, and the (3) pitchman, in that order.

Split 40 Defense Versus the Houston Veer Triple Option—When we attack the Houston Veer Triple Option off the Split 40 Defense, we use the same defensive assignments and techniques as used against the Sprint Out Option with the halfback dive attack. The most important difference between attacking these two options is that the outside linebacker or defensive end must be quicker to defend against the dive versus the Houston Veer, because the running back directs his course just to the outside of his offensive guard. Against the Sprint Out Option, the dive back sets a course usually outside of the offensive tackle rather than the offensive guard; otherwise, the Split 40 Defense attacks these two offensive attacks using the same defensive methods.

Split 40 Defense Versus the Outside Belly Option—Our defensive staff believes that each defender must be assigned men versus all option plays. Whenever the defenders are free to attack the ball, or who they believe has the ball, this is when the long gainer develops; therefore, most of our defenders have predetermined assigned men on all potential option plays. Specific linebackers are exceptions to this rule; some linebackers are assigned men at specific points of the attack (Diagram 6-42).

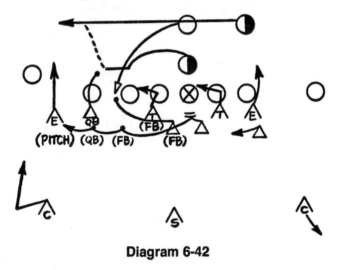

Diagram 6-42

When the outside belly maneuver develops toward the tight end side normally assigned the playside, the inside linebacker is assigned to scrape off and is assigned to stop the fullback. The defensive tackle plays through the head of the guard and then sets a course to help the linebacker on the fullback. The backside inside linebacker slides over head up on the center and checks for counters or traps and then scallops down the line checking for the fullback, the quarterback keeper, or the pitchman who is the backside halfback. The outside playside linebacker attacks the quarterback and the playside defensive end is responsible to contain the outside play if the quarterback makes the pitch (Diagram 6-42).

If the outside linebacker and defensive end to the side of the action have a cross deal on these two defenders, they change their defensive assignments. The end who knives in over the offensive end's original position knows he's assigned to attack the quarterback, while the linebacker, who crosses to the outside, is assigned to contain the option pitch (Diagram 6-43).

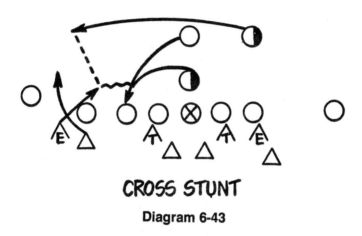

CROSS STUNT
Diagram 6-43

When the offense runs the belly option toward the short or split end side, the fullback is then assigned to both the defensive tackle and inside playside Split 40 linebacker. The end is assigned to attack the quarterback, while the outside linebacker is responsible for the pitchman. The reason for these assignments is that the outside linebacker may not only be stacked, but he may also be in his walk away or double cover position. This means from these two latter positions he must be in good position to stop the pitchman from breaking containment. It is easy to see this is his only possible assignment from a walk away or double cover alignment. Therefore, we stay with these normal outside belly assignments to the split end side (Diagram 6-44).

Split 40 Defense Versus the Texas (Wishbone) Triple Option—If the offense runs the Texas three back option to the tight end's side, we

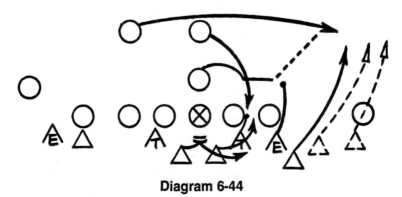

Diagram 6-44

also assign defenders to each member of the offensive option unit. Since the fullback must be stopped to force the quarterback to carry out the next two parts of his option, we assign the defensive tackle and outside linebacker to attack the fullback immediately. The inside frontside linebacker also is assigned to search the fullback before checking for the quarterback keeping the ball. The backside inside linebacker is assigned to check the fullback first, the quarterback second, and the pitchman as the third assignment. The strongside defensive end is assigned to contain the pitch, but he does not sprint right out to his outside. He is taught to "stare down" on the quarterback, trying to make the field general string out the option. He only attacks the quarterback when he is definitely sure the quarterback has kept the ball, and he would make the tackle on the signal caller downfield. Once the quarterback makes his pitch to the pitchman (backside halfback), the defensive end tries to string out the sweep so that the defensive pursuit will be able to cut off the ball carrier. The defensive end has to play off the lead blocker if he attempts to block the contain man. The end must never get knocked off his feet and must use his arms to ward off all potential blockers. If he can hold up and contain the pitchman only slightly, the deep safetyman and the outside playside cornerman should react to the option pitch (Diagram 6-45).

If the offense runs the triple option to the split end side, the defensive end and linebacker exchange their assignments as compared to their tight end's side assignments. The defensive stack to the split end side makes it necessary for the defensive end to attack the fullback, and the outside linebacker is then assigned to contain the quarterback's potential option pitch to the pitchman. The frontside inside linebacker is still assigned to scallop over to the flow of the offensive backfield, searching the fullback for the ball on the run. Again the inside frontside linebacker's main

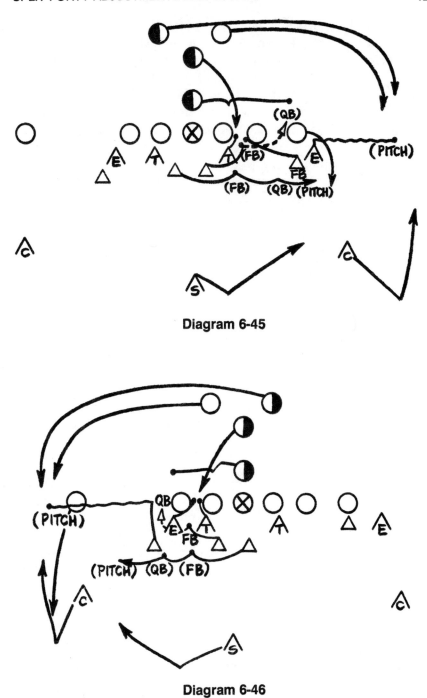

Diagram 6-45

Diagram 6-46

responsibility is to tackle the quarterback after he has made the pitch to the backside (left halfback) and pursue the ball (Diagram 6-46).

A defensive stunt by the defensive end and outside linebacker would exchange their defensive responsibilities by changing their offensive "man" assignments. This is also true if the frontside inside linebacker follows his predetermined team blitz and fires into the "1" gap, and then the defensive playside tackle stunts into the "3" gap. These two defenders' assignments are also altered because of the stunt called in the defensive huddle. Therefore, we have our basic methods of attacking the triple option and then a couple of stunting and blitzing variations to keep the optioning quarterback guessing.

Chapter 7

How to Teach the
Split Forty Defense

TEACHING SPLIT FORTY DEFENSIVE CONSISTENCY

For any team who desires winning consistency, a sound, attacking, hard-nosed defense is essential. All defensive units make mistakes; therefore, sound coaching and superior fundamental teaching minimize mistakes by eliminating individual erros. Our defense is a coordinated team defense in which every man must know his defensive alignments, techniques, and responsibilities. The defensive staff continually emphasizes that all champion defensive players must be aggressive, hard-nosed tacklers and make the big play in all clutch situations.

TEACHING PRIDE

The coach should expect nothing but the best from each defender. Defensive drills should emphasize quickness, hitting, reaction, pursuit, and pride. All defenders should strive to be the best in all drills and games. The coach should point out the outstanding performance as well as the poor performance. The poor performer's pride should be hurt to such an extent that he requests another chance to perform. A coach knows he has achieved defensive team pride when his defenders come out early or stay after practice to challenge one another in a particular drill.

TEACHING SUCCESS

Every defensive player must achieve some form of success in all drills. The main objective of all defensive drills is to instill confidence in each defender. If each player achieves success in each drill, it will build up his confidence as a quality defender. Once he has achieved this confidence, he will be mentally and physically ready to win the big game.

IN SEASON TEACHING TECHNIQUES

We put the pressure on our defenders during each practice session so that they will be able to "face the music" on Saturday. We do not continually lecture to our defensive players; we like to put the chalk in the players' hands. We teach tackling and defending against the pass every day in our practice sessions. Defensive groups meet with their position coach as much as possible. We believe in the theory that it is not important what the coach knows, but how much material the coach can teach to his players. The players receive a scouting report on the opposition's offensive program on Monday. On Tuesday, the players receive a tip sheet. On Wednesday, the players are given certain questions which they must answer, and the only way that they can obtain the correct answers is by viewing our opponent's film.

The defensive coaching staff wants all of the defenders to know every move employed by the opponent's offensive players against each specific defender. We teach our defenders how to read the offensive linemen he may face. For example, we teach the defender to read the heels of the offensive down lineman. If the down offensive lineman's heels are flat on the ground, it is almost certain that he will set up in a pass blocking technique; while if his heels are off the ground, it is almost a sure bet that the offensive man in a down position will fire out and show pass quickly.

At least three times each week our staff practices the correct pursuit channels or angles.

COACHING THE DEFENSIVE TACKLES "23"

Alignment: The defensive tackle should line up, splitting the outside foot of the offensive guard. The top of the helmet should be even with the outside shoulder of the guard (Diagrams 7-1 and 7-2).

Stance: Four point parallel stance with the feet slightly wider than the hands. Step with inside foot first.

Coaching Points: Charge through the neck and head of the guard with the inside foot. Penetrate one yard. Square shoulders to the line of scrimmage as soon as contact is made. Take away inside trap. Fight

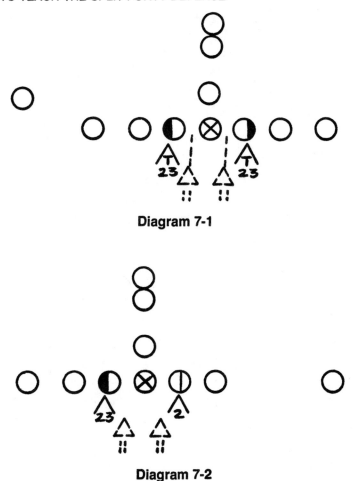

Diagram 7-1

Diagram 7-2

through pressure of guard's block. If tackle blocks down, deliver a blow with outside arm. Spin to outside only as last resort.

Keys:

1. Move on the guard's movement and blast through the guard. Don't let the guard block the inside linebacker.
2. Stop the opponent's trap by keeping shoulders parallel to the line of scrimmage and use anti-trap technique by taking on the trapper. Drop the inside shoulder and get lower than the trapper. Fight pressure and squeeze down to minimize the trap hole.
3. If the guard pulls toward the tackle, be ready to fight the

pressure of the tackle's block. Spin out only as a last resort off the outside foot, staying as close to the line of scrimmage as possible. Stay low and dip the inside shoulder—don't let the blocker get to your legs!

4. If the guard pulls toward the center, close down and cut off the ball carrier. Take a flat pursuit course.

Adjustments:

To Split End Side:

1. Move closer to the guard; at times we will use a "2" position.
2. Always use a squared up alignment.

Versus a Man In Motion:

1. Slide call puts tackle away from motion in squared up "2" position.
2. Slide call puts tackle in squared up position to the side of motion.

Reaction:

1. If straight back pocket pass shows, the tackle should attack directly over the head of the guard. He should execute a relative rush, staying in his correct lane. Don't get blocked inside.
2. He should keep the blocker away from his body on a pass rush. He must use his hands to ward off the blockers and get his arms up high, to obstruct the passer's vision, just as the passer sets to throw.
3. The defensive tackle should never let the offensive guard drive him outside or get hooked in by the blocker (Diagrams 7-1 and 7-2).

Four Point Parallel Defensive Line Stance: The defender lines up in a parallel four point stance with the feet the width of the armpits, in a parallel stance with the weight on the balls of the feet. His hands are directly in front of the feet, and the knees and ankles are bent over the defender's toes. The butt and the shoulders should be even, and the head should be relaxed. The eyes should be focused on the key defender's hands in a four point stance.

The depth off the line of scrimmage depends upon our game plan, score, time, weather conditions, down, distance, and the ability and experience of our down linemen.[1]

DEFENSIVE TACKLE "23" REACTIONS

Position: The defensive tackle should line up, splitting the outside foot of the offensive guard.

Initial Movement and Execution: The tackle should explode into the offensive guard, using the inside forearm and stepping with the inside or same foot. The defender should try to keep the offensive guard off the linebacker. The defender should read the tackle and fight pressure and then pursue the ball carrier.

Responsibility: The defender should anchor the off-tackle hole and fight the pressure of the offensive blocking scheme.

1. If play toward: Fight pressure of block and pursue from an inside-out angle.
2. If play away: Fight pressure of block, read and take flat pursuit course to reach the ball carrier.
3. Drop back pocket pass: Rush intelligently using the relative rush assignment by staying in the prescribed rushing lane. Maintain the relative relationship to the near side defensive end and the other defensive tackle.

DEFENSIVE TACKLE ADJUSTMENTS AND TECHNIQUES (SPLIT 40 DEFENSE)

The basic move by the defensive tackle in his "23" alignment is through the guard's head. His responsibility is to keep the offensive guard off his inside linebacker, and he must never be hooked or turned out by the offensive guard (Diagram 7-3).

If the offensive guard pulls across the center's head, the defensive tackle is coached to close down hard and penetrate one yard and then pursue and tackle the ball carrier (Diagram 7-4).

---

[1]*Coaching Note:* We like the parallel defensive tackle's stance rather than the "turned in" or "angled in" stance used by the Notre Dame defensive tackles of the '60s. The parallel stance enables the defensive tackles to move more freely in any direction to meet the ball carrier with the shoulders parallel to the line of scrimmage and gives the defender a more panoramic view of the potential offensive blockers. The parallel stance also allows the defensive tackle an unlimited pursuit range in any direction to cut off the ball carrier. This squared up parallel stance eliminates the blind side employed by the old "turned in" or "angled in" defensive tackle stance.

Diagram 7-3

Diagram 7-4

Diagram 7-5

When the guard pulls across the tackle's face, the defensive tackle should check the inside for the trap first, and then look for the fold block by the offensive tackle. If the defensive tackle feels pressure, he should be ready to spin out as shallow to the line of scrimmage as possible. This technique is only used as a last resort (Diagram 7-5).

Against the short or split end side, the defensive tackle moves closer inside toward the offensive guard. He may also assume a parallel head up stance ("2" alignment, Diagram 7-6).

At other times when using the Split 40 Defense, a tackle control method is used to line up the defensive tackle in a "21" technique. This alignment places the defensive tackle inside of the offensive guard by making the tackle split the inside foot of the offensive guard. Usually along with this "21" technique, the inside Split 40 linebacker moves out

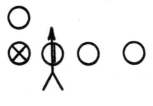

Diagram 7-6

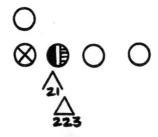

Diagram 7-7

Diagram 7-8

from his customary "11" technique to a "223" alignment (Diagram 7-7).

Another method of using tackle control is to line up in the 40 Pro Defense. The middle linebacker now controls the defensive tackles who line up using their usual "2" technique, but now the middle linebacker may call the tackles to stunt to one side or the other of the offensive guards. This means the middle lienbacker fills the open hole. The middle linebacker controls these tackles by an In or Out call (Diagram 7-8).

DEFENSIVE TACKLE'S STRONG SIDE ALIGNMENT

As previously noted, the defensive tackle away from the flanker or formation side will usually line up in his customary "23" technique (two tight ends). The defensive tackle's responsibility to the side of the flanker or formation may change slightly toward the flanker in both alignment and technique, depending upon our game plan.

Responsibility of Defensive Tackle to Flanker's Side: At times we may line the defensive tackle up in the gap between the guard and the tackle (3 gap). On the snap of the ball, the defender is coached to fire through the "3" gap on all fours and penetrate to a depth of the original position of the offensive lineman's feet. Once he reaches this point, he should stay low in a balanced position and react to the ball (Diagram 7-9). Another technique that may be used by the defensive tackle to the flanker's side is to fire out into the offensive tackle's near shoulder-neck area and read as he goes (Diagram 7-10).

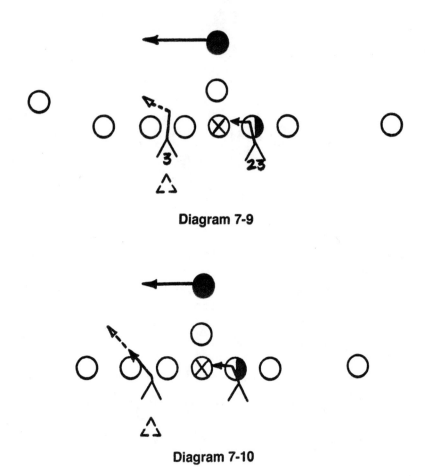

Diagram 7-9

Diagram 7-10

DEFENSIVE TACKLE DRILLS (SPLIT FORTY DEFENSE)

The following three drills are our favorite teaching methods to coach the defender to defeat the offensive block, fight pressure, and attack the ball carrier.

Tackle's Reaction Drills (Diagram 7-11):

TACKLE REACTION DRILL
Diagram 7-11

Objective: React to the block the defender will face in the game.

Organization: Five offensive players lined up in tackle, guard, and center positions. Two defensive tackles in normal alignment. Coach may play quarterback.

Execution: Defensive tackle moves on movement and either delivers a blow on the offensive blocker or reacts to the offensive blocker's course. Defensive tackle must learn to fight pressure, make the correct pursuit course, and keep his shoulders parallel to the line of scrimmage as he approaches the ball carrier.

Coaching Points: Coach should check stance, movement, explosion, fight pressure, read and pursuit.

One on Three Drill (Diagrams 7-12, 7-13, 7-14, 7-15, 7-16, 7-17):

Objective: Develop the correct reactions for a defender keying and reading three offensive linemen.

Organization: Coach stands behind defender facing the offensive linemen and signals, by hand, starting count and blocking patterns for all three blockers. Manager or extra defensive lineman may act as ball carrier.

Execution: Coach signals three blockers to use the following techniques:

    a. Fold block (Diagram 7-12)
    b. Double team block (Diagram 7-13)

TACKLE REACTION DRILL
Diagram 7-12

TACKLE REACTION DRILL
Diagram 7-13

TACKLE REACTION DRILL
Diagram 7-14

TACKLE REACTION DRILL

Diagram 7-15

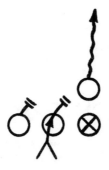

TACKLE REACTION DRILL

Diagram 7-16

TACKLE REACTION DRILL

Diagram 7-17

    c. Reach block (Diagram 7-14)

    d. Step around block (Diagram 7-15)

    e. Pass block (Diagram 7-16)

    f. Pull away block (Diagram 7-17)

Coaching Points: Emphasize alignment, stance, and reactions.

   Middle Four Drill (Diagram 7-18):

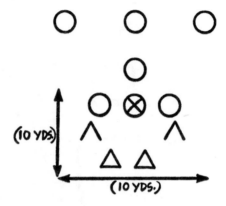

MIDDLE FOUR DRILL

Diagram 7-18

Objective: Offense vs. Defense. Offense is given three downs to gain ten yards. Defense must stop them.

Organization: Four interior defenders versus seven-man offensive unit within a ten by ten square.

Execution: Offense runs interior attack at the defense and is given three downs to make ten yards. The ball carrier runs hand-off drills but can break off his course at will. This makes the defender play honest. The defenders must execute moving on movement, deliver a blow, fight pressure, pursue, and gang tackle. This is a highly competitive drill with offense cheering for offense and defense cheering for their defenders. A whistle is used to end the drill.

Coaching Points: Emphasize the defender going through the head of the blocker and taking the correct pursuit angle to the ball carrier (Diagram 7-18).

COACHING THE DEFENSIVE INSIDE LINEBACKER "11"

Alignment: Inside linebackers should split the center-guard gap. Alignment should be an arm's length from the tackle's heels (Diagrams 7-19 and 7-20).

Stance: Two point stance with the inside leg up and the outside leg back.

Coaching Point: The linebackers should make sure the offensive guard cannot get into their feet.

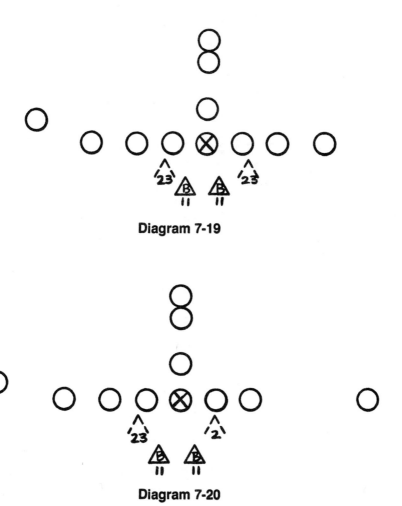

Diagram 7-19

Diagram 7-20

Keys: Basic action keys:

1. Action To: The linebacker must scallop gaining ground into the off-tackle hole. He should never get tied up by his defensive tackle. The "11" defender must not let the center or guard block him. He must stay about two feet behind the ball so he does not overrun the ball carrier.
2. Action Away: The linebacker is taught to shuffle head up on the center, keeping his shoulders parallel to the line of scrimmage. Check for the counter or trap up the middle.
3. Play Action Pass To: Attack the area of responsibility or take the hook pass responsibility, depending upon the defensive call.
4. Play Action Pass Away: Drop back to the direction of the near safetyman. Level off as soon as the quarterback sets up.
5. Straight Drop Back Pass: Sprint back to the hook area.

Adjustments: Adjustments may be made on a game to game basis.

TEACHING THE INSIDE SPLIT 40 LINEBACKER "11"

Stance: The linebacker should line up with his feet and shoulders parallel to the line of scrimmage. The feet should be lined up directly below the backer's armpits. The butt should be dropped with the shoulders parallel to the line of scrimmage and the back should be straight. The head should be up with the arms hanging relaxed just inside the knees (Diagram 7-21).

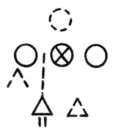

Diagram 7-21

Alignment: Line up in an "11" technique, directly in front of the center-guard gap two to three yards off the line of scrimmage (Diagram 7-21).

Key: Key the ball first and then read the blocking pattern of the offensive tackle, guard, and center. As the ball moves, the inside linebacker should move. He should stay on the line if the ball stays on the line and gain depth as the ball gains depth. The quarterback's three basic moves are: (1) reverse out (Diagram 7-22), (2) sprint out (Diagram 7-23), and (3) open up (Diagram 7-24).

Diagram 7-22

Diagram 7-23

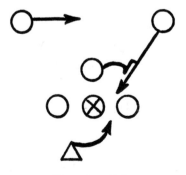

Diagram 7-24

Responsibility:

1. If drop back pass shows, drop back into the hook zone (Diagram 7-25).

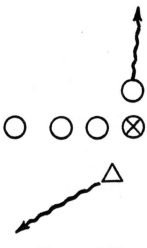

Diagram 7-25

2. Action To: Scrape off outside of the defensive tackle. Protect the off-tackle area and keep the shoulders parallel to the line of scrimmage in order to react in any direction the ball carrier may select (Diagram 7-26).

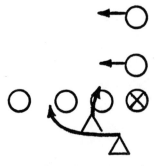

Diagram 7-26

3. Action Away: Check the center area for a possible cutback or counter maneuver and then pursue the ball (Diagram 7-27).

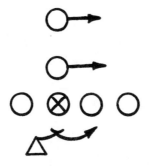

Diagram 7-27

4. Sprint or Roll Out To: Scrape off and attack the play action pass if committed. If not, drop to hook zone (Diagram 7-28).

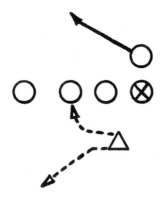

Diagram 7-28

5. Sprint Out Pass Away: Check center for possible draw and then drop back. Direction of drop depends upon the direction and lateral movement of the ball. As soon as the passer sets up, the backside linebacker should gain depth (Diagram 7-29). If an opening appears over the center, the linebacker may blitz.

As the linebacker scrapes or wipes off, he should work upfield over the outside shoulder of his defensive tackle. He should keep his shoulders parallel to the line of scrimmage, keeping the outside leg and arm free as he steps into the off-tackle hole (Diagram 7-30). Scrape as tight to the tackle as possible.

After scraping off, the linebacker is coached to rush through any opening. If there is no opening, he may have to bump or shuffle up the line of scrimmage until an opening presents itself (Diagram 7-31).

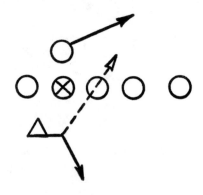

Diagram 7-29

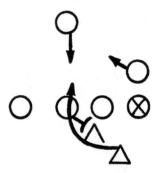

Diagram 7-30

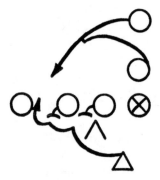

Diagram 7-31

He should look for the offensive end to block down and meet him with the outside forearm and the outside leg. Keep the shoulders parallel to the line of scrimmage. This may happen even though the outside strong linebacker is assigned the task of keeping the offensive end off the inside scraping linebacker. Fight the pressure of the end's block, locate the ball, and take the proper pursuit course to cut off the ball carrier (Diagram 7-32).

Diagram 7-32

If the play goes directly at the inside linebacker, he must be ready to meet with pressure. Step up to the inside with the inside foot and deliver a blow with the inside forearm. Stay low and attack the ball carrier (Diagram 7-33). Keep the shoulders parallel to the line of scrimmage.

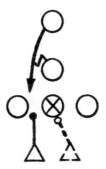

Diagram 7-33

LINEBACKER'S TECHNIQUES

Scraping or Wiping Off Technique—Flow To: The linebacker is coached to take a short lead step with his outside foot at a thirty-five degree angle, head upfield, and then take a crossover step with the inside foot directed at the original position of the defensive tackle's outside foot. The linebacker is coached to watch the offensive line's blocking pattern and to use his inside forearm or shiver to keep his shoulders parallel to the goal line. The inside wiping or scraping linebacker should stay on the ball carrier's hip (or slightly behind him) so that the defender will be in excellent position if the ball carrier decides to cut back and break a run back against the grain. The scraping linebacker must be ready to give ground slightly, using a scalloping technique so he does not get cut off from the offensive end or any other outside offensive blocker. If the offensive tackle attempts to block the inside linebacker from the outside, the "1" defender is coached to drive over and through the blocker (Diagram 7-34).

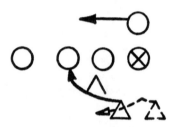

Diagram 7-34

The inside linebacker is taught to attack the ball from an inside-out angle. If a play action pass shows, the inside linebacker should continue to follow through with his wipe off technique and attack the passer. If a drop back pass shows quickly, the inside linebacker is coached to drop back quickly to his hook zone responsibility. As he drops back to his hook zone responsibility, he must be aware of a potential draw play. If a draw play develops, he is responsible to call out "Draw!" and react to the play.

Scraping or Wiping Off Technique—Flow Away: As soon as flow goes away, the backside inside "11" linebacker is coached to check the center for any counter, reverse, or cutback plays. The backside linebacker is coached to butt the center in the numbers with his helmet, and use his two hand shiver to keep the center away from his feet. As soon as he locates the ball, he should shed the center and keep his shoulders parallel to the goal line. He should hold for a count of 1,001, check for counters or traps, and then pursue the ball carrier from his inside-out angle. If a play action shows, the backside inside linebacker is taught to drop back into his hook zone. If a quick drop back pass shows, the inside linebacker should ignore the offensive center and sprint quickly back into his respective hook zone. As he drops back into his defensive pass area, he should be alert for a possible draw pass. If a draw play develops, he should call it out and react to the ball carrier (Diagram 7-35).

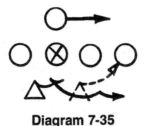

Diagram 7-35

Linebacker's Scrape Off Technique Versus Offensive Fold Block: If the opposition employs the flood block between the offensive guard and tackle, we like to scrape off quickly with our linebacker in order to beat the offensive guard stepping around the offensive tackle's block. As soon as the linebacker shoots through the gap in the offensive line, he must locate the ball. If the ball is going away from the scraping linebacker, he is taught to use his level-off technique, which flattens his course so that he will be able to cut off the ball carrier on or near the line of scrimmage (Diagram 7-36).

Diagram 7-36

Coaching the Linebacker to Deliver a Blow (Two Point Stance): In teaching the basic fundamentals of delivering a blow from the two point position, we use the two man and seven man sleds. Next, we use a reaction machine with two arms that can flip forward when triggered by the coach, and then we use a large swinging dummy. Both our defensive ends and linebackers basically use a two point stance so we emphasize the forearm blow, stepping with the same foot and delivering a forearm blow with the same arm. The main coaching point is to teach the defender to lock his elbow and hit the dummy with a lift. The defender must synchronize a quick short step and an explosive blow. Each defender works from both his left and right side, keeping his shoulders parallel to the line of scrimmage. Next, we teach the defender to get rid of the blocker or the swing bag with his opposite hand. Once the defender has mastered the forearm blow and is able to get rid of the bag, we have him scallop down the line and tackle a dummy or a ball carrier.

Common Faults in Delivering a Blow: The most common fault in delivering a blow for most defenders is taking too large a step, which minimizes the blow and enables the blocker to tie up the defender. The next problem is stepping with the opposite foot of the forearm with which the defender is delivering the blow. The third most common fault is when the defender tries to wind up to deliver a blow. The wind-up takes too much time and limits the defender's chance of keeping his shoulders parallel to the line of scrimmage, so that he is able to pursue in any direction.

Again the coach should watch each individual deliver a blow and look for the three most common faults: first, overstriding; second, stepping with the opposite foot of the forearm blow; third, the blocker attempting to wind up to deliver a blow.

The reader may question the continual reference and emphasis upon delivering a blow with the same foot, same arm. The main reason for this coaching point is that we constantly stress to our outside linebackers and defensive ends to hide their outside foot and keep their outside arm free to get rid of the blocker or to fight off an outside block. Therefore, our outside backers and defensive ends step with their inside foot and deliver a blow with their inside arm so that the blocker is unable to hook the outside leg of the defender. Once the blocker is able to get into the outside defender's leg, the defender does not have adequate time to recover and attack the outside offensive attack.

Coaching the Linebacker Versus the Run and the Pass: Quick, hard-nosed, and agile linebackers are the backbone of any successful defensive unit. The linebacker unit must be flexible because these defenders must split their time between both the running and passing game. Therefore, the linebackers must be tough enough to make a good sting on a running back and must be quick enough to defend against the pass. A prerequisite of any good linebacker is quick feet. Linebackers must be able to attack the ball at the point of the attack, straight ahead, or from sideline to sideline. The linebacker must also be quick enough to sprint backward and intercept the pass in the hook, flat, or curl area.

LINEBACKER'S FOOTBALL KNOWLEDGE

A linebacker must have football sense and have the feel for what the opposition is going to do before the ball is put into play. He must be a team man and play team defense. He must not try to react as an individual. He must be a hitter and have the speed and quickness to get to the ball carrier and then punish him with a solid tackle. A linebacker must have good eyes and be able to pick up the ball carrier immediately after coming off a block. He must have the desire and the spirit to be the best defender at his position. The linebacker must be able to defend himself from any type of an offensive block. There are times when any linebacker may be blocked, but he must never stay blocked. He must be able to recognize the type of block, fight pressure, and free himself of the block. If he is ever knocked off his feet, he must bounce back to his feet, as quickly as possible, and take the correct pursuit course for the ball carrier. Rebounding to his feet is one defensive technique we practice every day. We tell our defenders that they may get blocked at times, but they must never stay blocked!

We teach our linebackers to constantly move around prior to the snap of the ball. We tell our linebackers to use as many defensive looks as possible, but we try to keep the linebacker technique to a minimum.

STANCE AND COURSE OF SPLIT LINEBACKERS

Scallop Course: The frontside inside Split 40 linebacker is coached to take a short forty-five degree lead step up and toward the line of scrimmage. The next step is a longer step with the backside foot, and the next step is with the outside foot (Diagram 7-37). Once the linebacker

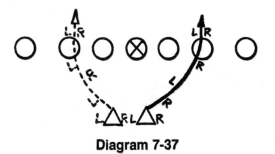

Diagram 7-37

decides he is going to attack across the line of scrimmage, he should have his shoulders squared to the line of scrimmage. The backside inside linebacker should begin his lateral movement in the direction of the offensive quarterback's route. His first checkpoint is to make sure the offense does not run a counter play over the offensive center (Diagram 7-37).

Split Forty Inside Linebacker's Lateral Movement:

1. **Lateral Start**—Linebacker should take a short forty-five degree lead step (three to four inches) with the near foot, in the direction of his key. Step with backside foot in front of lead step. As linebacker steps with the backside foot, he should push off lead foot and use backside arm in a powerful thrust in the direction of the key.

2. **Scallop Course**—The scallop course is a lateral up-in-back course used by the linebacker. He steps up-in at each hole that the ball carrier fakes into. (Scallop drill emphasizes the linebacker's correct scallop course.) The linebacker must keep his shoulders parallel to the line of scrimmage and be careful not to overrun the ball carrier. He should stay on the hip of the ball carrier.

3. **Sprinting Laterally**—The linebacker sprints down the line of scrimmage to cut off the ball carrier. He does not scallop up and in but sprints under control. He must stay under control so he will be in a good football position if the ball carrier is forced to cut back into the pursuing linebacker. This is more of a shuffling technique.

4. **Changing Lateral Direction**—The linebacker should scallop or sprint under balanced control so that he may change direction if an offensive counter or reverse maneuver forces the linebacker to change his route. To change direction, the linebacker should plant the lead foot, shift the weight toward his back foot, and take a short three to four inch step with the backside foot in the opposite direction. Therefore, the linebackers should be forced to take smaller controlled steps when pursuing the flow of the offensive backs. (The Defensive Wave Drills are excellent teaching drills to coach the change of lateral direction.)

DEFENSIVE INSIDE LINEBACKER DRILLS
(SPLIT FORTY DEFENSE)

The defensive coaching staff uses the following three defensive drills to teach the inside Split 40 linebacker how to move on movement, deliver a blow, fight pressure, pursue, and gang tackle. We teach the forearm blow and the two arm shiver. The two arm shiver is used when the linebacker has to scallop down the line of scrimmage.

Deliver the Blow Drill (One on One):

Objective: Teaching progression of delivering a blow.

Organization: One blocker, one defender; coach points direction.

Execution: Defender should look directly at the blocker and deliver the blow at the blocker's numbers. The defender should step up and use the same foot and the same arm. The defender should throw his hips into the explosion. The feet should be balanced and accelerating upon contact. The forearm should be an upward and outward blast. The backside arm should move to rid the blocker, just as the defender begins his follow through of the forearm blast. Coach then points in the direction the defender should slide toward.

Coaching Points: Defender should put *everything* into the forearm explosion (Diagram 7-38).

DELIVER THE BLOW DRILL

Diagram 7-38

Inside Split 40 Linebacker's Reaction Drill:

Objective: React to the block or movement of the ball carrier.

Organization: Offensive center, guards, and quarterback. Four dummies can replace the offensive tackles and ends.

Execution: Inside linebackers should key the ball and slide or scallop in the direction of the ball. At times, the backside linebacker may be told to fire into the frontside "11" gap and attack the sprint out or sweep from the backside. Good drill to run counter action plays.

Coaching Points: Linebackers should never overrun the ball. They should sprint back to their respective hook zones, with their heads on a swivel, on a straight drop back pass (Diagram 7-39).

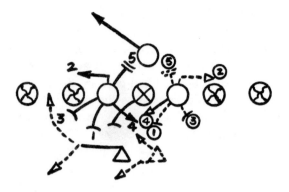

SPLIT 40 LINEBACKER REACTION DRILL
Diagram 7-39

Half Line Drill:

Objective: Teach defenders strong or weak side of opponent's attack, to stop opposition's favorite plays.

Organization: Line up center and all other offensive linemen to his left or right and add four offensive backs. The defense uses its alignment corresponding to the offensive unit.

Execution: The offensive attack runs its bread and butter plays from cards drawn up from the scouting reports and film breakdowns. Blockers and ball carrier emulate same techniques used by the next opponent.

Coaching Points: Drill is run thud or live, and defensive coach must stress correct defensive execution. Coach may use down, distance, yard line and hash marks to lend authenticity to the drill. This is an excellent unit drill to develop defensive pride, execution, and enthusiasm (Diagram 7-40).

COACHING THE DEFENSIVE ENDS "6" AND "8"

Alignment: The end's inside foot should be two to three feet outside of the offensive end (Diagrams 7-41 and 7-42).

Stance: Two point stance with the inside leg up and the outside leg back.

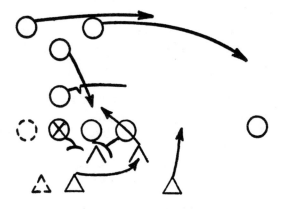

HALF-LINE DRILL

Diagram 7-40

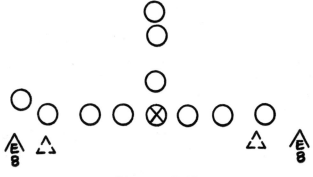

Diagram 7-41

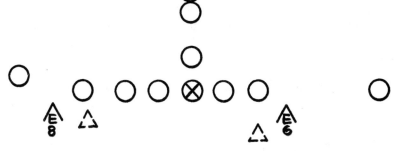

Diagram 7-42

Coaching Points: Move on movement and attack defender on the third step with the inside leg and the inside arm. Use hands if the blocker scrambles for the feet. You are the contain man.

End Keys Halfback:

1. If halfback comes straight at you, keep outside leverage and deliver a blow with the inside arm.
2. If halfback tries to use a turn-out block, close down through his outside shoulder.
3. If halfback tries to use a hook block, scramble to the outside and beat the blocker.

End's Basic Assignment Versus:

1. Triple Option = Take quarterback
2. Inside Belly = Take ball
3. Outside Belly = Take quarterback
4. Power Sweep = Take ball
5. Sprint Out = Take ball
6. Sprint Out Option = Take quarterback (cat and mouse)
7. Action Away = Watch for reverses, counters, and bootleg
8. Roll Out Pass Action = Attack from Outside-In
9. Pocket Pass = Attack from Outside-In Rush through the passer, contain

Split End: The end's assignment is the same to the split side. If run, force the football; if pass, contain the pass. Check the outside linebacker's call for any change of assignments.

THE SPLIT FORTY WIDE DEFENSE

The basic difference between the Split 40 Wide Defense and our Split 40 Defense is basically the alignment and play of the defensive end and outside linebacker. The Wide Split 40 alignment places the defensive end in a wider "8" alignment.

Defensive End: The technique for the wide defensive end is to line up about two and one-half feet outside of the offensive end. Use a two or three point stance with the outside foot back. The defender's inside hand should be down in a three point stance, and he may be angled inward watching for the near back. The first step should be a quick shuffle step with the inside foot and then a short step with the outside foot. The third step should bring the defender across the line of scrimmage on a slight inside angle, with the inside leg forward and ready to deliver a blow with the inside arm, destroying the blocker. The defensive end is assigned to contain the wide plays and to close down, thus cutting off the funnel or seam between the defensive end and the linebacker. This is referred to as the "squeeze" or the force-contain technique.

When lining up to the split end's side, the wide end lines up in a "45" or outside shoulder position on the defensive tackle or a "4" alignment if the outside linebacker lines up inside of the defensive end.

Outside Defensive Linebacker: The outside linebacker lines up normally on the inside shoulder of the offensive end "65" technique. This alignment may change to a head up position on the offensive tight end (66), to a walk away position to the split end side, to a stack directly behind the defensive end or two yards outside of the defensive end.

The outside defensive linebacker must be ready to deliver a blow into the offensive end and get rid of him, and attack the ball if it comes his way. If a sprint out pass develops to his side, he must be ready to attack the quarterback or defend against the pass, depending upon the defensive call. If a sprint out pass develops away from his position, he must be alert for a throw back pass. If the opponent runs a play away from the outside linebacker, he must be ready to chase or take a proper pursuit angle on the ball, depending upon the defensive call. Therefore, the outside linebacker reads the offensive tackle-end-near back triangle when he lines up on the inside shoulder of the tight end (Diagram 7-43).

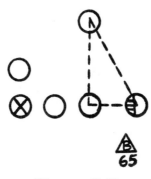

Diagram 7-43

The alignments and assignments of the defensive end and outside linebacker are covered versus two wide men (Diagram 7-44) and 7-45). How to cover a wing back up to two yards is illustrated in Diagram 7-46. The wing back at three yards is drawn up in Diagram 7-47. The flanker at

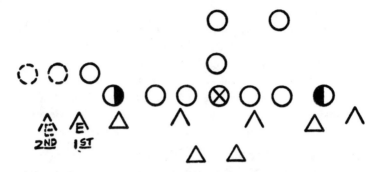

E
2ND
E
1ST
END/VERSUS- ONE OR TWO WIDE MEN-
PLAY ONE OR TWO POSITIONS.

Diagram 7-44

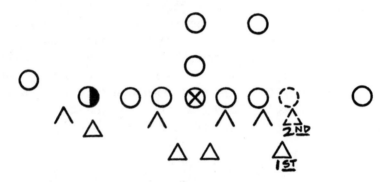

2ND
1ST
LB/VERSUS-ONE OR TWO WIDE MEN-
PLAY ONE OR TWO POSITIONS.

Diagram 7-45

(1YD.) (2 YDS.)
B
E
E
UP TO TWO YARDS

Diagram 7-46

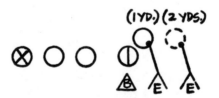

AT THREE YARDS

Diagram 7-47

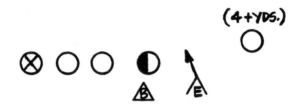

OVER FOUR YARDS END MUST BE FLANKER ACROSS LINE

Diagram 7-48

IF END CAN NOT BEAT FLANKER ACROSS LINE – PLAY INTO FLANKER.

Diagram 7-49

SWITCH VERSUS NASTY SPLIT

Diagram 7-50

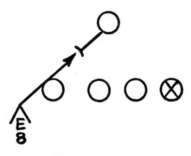

Diagram 7-51

Diagram 7-52

Diagram 7-53

four yards is diagrammed in Diagram 7-48. The head up and the switch positions of both the wide defensive end and outside linebacker are illustrated in Diagrams 7-49 and 7-50.

Therefore, as the reader can see in Diagrams 7-51 and 7-52, both the outside linebacker and end's positions are interchangeable, and it depends upon the defensive game plan as to who will play the outside or the inside position. This is also true of the defensive rules versus the wing back and flanker set and the End's Split Rule in the following pages.

DEFENSIVE END ("8") TECHNIQUE

The defensive end is coached to move on the offensive end's movement and to shoot for a target area two yards behind the offensive end. As the defensive end nears his target area, he is coached to look for the near back. If the near back attempts to block the defender, the "8" defender is taught to step low, deliver a blow, and hold his ground. This type of aggressive end play plugs up the off-tackle hole and also places the end in excellent position to rush any play action passes (Diagram 7-51).

On all drop back or pocket passes, the defensive end always rushes and has no defensive pass coverage responsibilities. He is responsible to rush and contain all drop back and sprint out passes his way. If the quarterback sprints out away from the rushing end, he is coached to trail the quarterback and put the pressure on him with a strong backside rush. Generally, the defensive end has the pitchman on option plays on his side unless he is involved in some type of a stunt

Wing Back-Flanker Rule: The defensive end is taught to line up on the outside shoulder of the one yard or normal wing back (Diagram 7-52). If the wing back splits out to two or three yards, the defensive end lines up his nose on the wing back (Diagram 7-52). When the wing back lines up four yards wide in a nasty type of a split, we teach the defensive end to move back to his normal "8" position. If the wing back moves out to more than four yards, the defensive end will then move in to the regular one to one and one-half yards outside of the offensive end. The outside linebacker may tell the end to switch positions, and then the linebacker uses the same split rule as illustrated in Diagram 7-52.

End's Split Rule: As soon as the offensive end moves out more than two yards, the defensive linebacker *may* knock the defensive end down to the outside shoulder of the offensive tackle. Then, the outside linebacker will line up head up on the split end up to two yards (Diagram 7-53). At three yards, the linebacker will go to the inside shoulder of the split end.

If the offensive end splits out more than three yards, the linebacker and end may return to their normal Split Forty alignment (Diagram 7-53).

Defensive End's Steps: Drive for a target spot one to one and one-half yards behind the tight end's original position. Attack at a forty-five degree angle aiming to the original position of the halfback. Attack the block with shoulders squared to the goal.

Step with the inside, outside, inside foot, and then shuffle step both feet parallel tothe line of scrimmage and look for an inside-out block by the near back or pulling lineman. Bend the inside knee and protect this inside foot with the inside forearm. Hide the outside leg and keep the shoulders parallel to the line of scrimmage (Diagram 7-54).

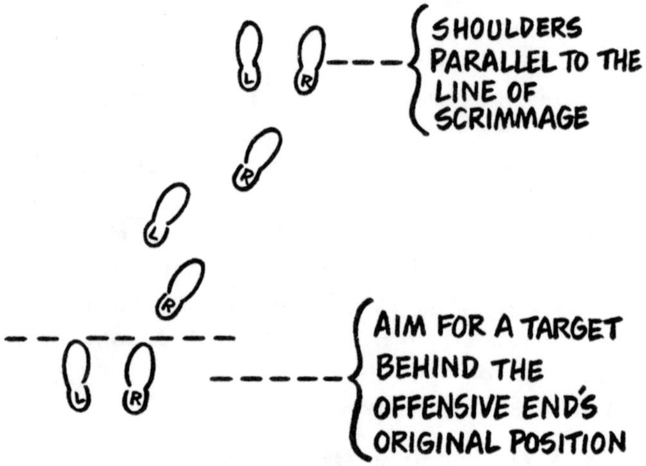

SHOULDERS PARALLEL TO THE LINE OF SCRIMMAGE

AIM FOR A TARGET BEHIND THE OFFENSIVE END'S ORIGINAL POSITION

Diagram 7-54

The defensive end must first be ready to explode into the blocker with the same leg, same arm, and force-contain the play if it comes toward the defensive end. If the play goes away, the end must be ready to chase the ball until the ball crosses the line of scrimmage, and then he is coached to take the proper pursuit course to cut off the ball carrier. Contain rush all passes. The defensive end must constantly practice his correct attack route and read on the run.

DEFENSIVE END'S DRILLS (SPLIT FORTY DEFENSE)

Both the End's Reaction Drill (Diagram 7-55) and the Perimeter Drill (Diagram 7-56) are excellent drills to teach the wide end ("8"

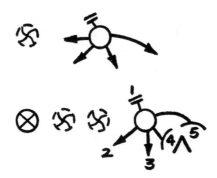

END'S REACTION DRILL

Diagram 7-55

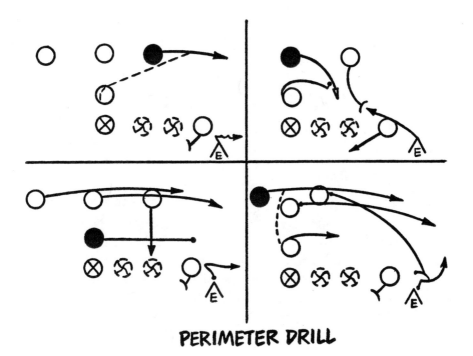

PERIMETER DRILL

Diagram 7-56

technique) how to react to the end's block and the offensive backfield action. The Defensive Chair Drill (Diagram 7-57) is an excellent drill to use to review defensive alignments, techniques, and stunts. The Defensive Chair Drill may be used by any defensive set, and it is a fine relaxing drill to use as a review the night before the game.

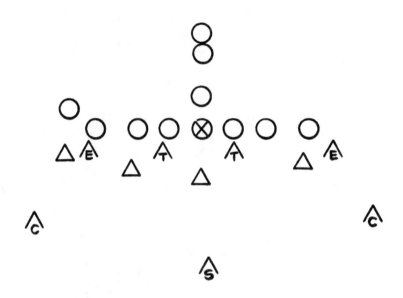

DEFENSIVE CHAIR DRILL

Diagram 7-57

End's Reaction Drill:

Objective: React to blocks defender will face in the game.

Organization: An offensive end, fullback, and blocking back versus a defensive end.

Execution: Defensive end moves on movement of the offensive end. His key is the near back through the offensive end. He delivers a blow or reacts to the offensive end and blocking back's course. The defender must explode into the end and make the proper pursuit course to attack the ball carrier. He must also be coached to use the correct chase course and look for any counters or reverses.

Coaching Points: Coach can check chase course movement, explosion, fight pressure and pursuit course (Diagram 7-55).

Perimeter Drill:

Objective: Teach wide defender on the line of scrimmage to read the course of the near back.

Organization: A complete offensive backfield versus two defenders.

Execution: Defensive man reacts to the block or the course of the near back. The defender must react to the play and pursue or chase the play, depending on the path of the ball carrier.

Coaching Points: The coach should stress delivering the blow, shuffling, and getting rid of the blocker as quickly as possible (Diagram 7-56).

Defensive Chair Drill:

Objective: Review defensive alignments and stunts in relaxed manner.

Organization: First team defense lines up eleven chairs and second liners line up in opposition's offensive sets.

Execution: The defensive signal caller calls a stunt from the defense's normal alignment, and the defense points to their assigned movement or stunts. Coach may ask a particular technique used by a specific defender if the opposition uses a fold or trap block. The defender then explains his technique verbally.

Coaching Points: An excellent drill to review assignments for the defensive unit without tiring the defenders. Helps keep the defenders mentally sharp. This drill is usually used at a team meeting the night before each game (Diagram 7-57).

TACKLE WITH THE SHOULDERS PARALLEL
TO THE GOAL LINE

All of our defenders are taught to stay as low as possible, keeping the shoulders parallel to the line of scrimmage. All defenders, when tackling, are taught to keep their helmets lower than the offensive helmets. On all "must" situations, we emphasize the ball carrier must never fall forward for needed yardage. The defenders are coached to make sure the ball carrier's helmet is pointed toward the opponent's goal line when the whistle blows and the dust disappears.

TACKLING (HEAD ON)

Purpose: Drive the ball carrier backward and bring him down.

Stance: Proper football position. The defender's shoulders should be parallel to the line of scrimmage and lower than the ball carrier's shoulders. Keep the head up and the tail low.

Approach: Aim the forehead for the bottom of the numbers. Maintain a bull neck, tail low, back straight, and head up. The eyes should always be focused on the target area.

Contact: The defender is coached to hit the runner with the forehead, wrap the arms around the ball carrier, and hug him. The tackler should squeeze the ball carrier and continue to drive and rise upward. Keep the feet moving, using short, choppy steps.

Follow Through: Hit and lift the ball carrier off his feet. Keep the feet chopping and drive the ball carrier backward and take him to the ground. The ball carrier's head should be pointed downfield, toward the opposition's goal line.

HOW TO COACH TACKLING

Tackling is not just a physical technique; it must also be a mental task to know how to accomplish the best technique on a given occasion, and it is also emotional because the defender must be ready to get the job done. The fundamentals of tackling must be reviewed each day.

A good hitter keeps his tail down and his eyes glued on the ball carrier. Good hitters are knee benders; therefore, we coach our tacklers to tackle through the ball carrier, attacking him from a low plane to a high plane. The tackler's arms must be thrust upward and then wrap the arms around the ball carrier so hard that his helmet will pop off! The knees should be bent on contact, then the legs should lift the ball carrier; then, continue driving until the whistle blows the ball dead.

If the tackler is making a sideline tackle, the head should always shoot across the ball carrier's body so that he can make a solid hit with the shoulder, and the forehead should pop the ball loose. The head should always lead on all tackles. On the head on tackle, the head leads first and is aimed at the ball carrier's numbers; but, as soon as contact is made, the ball carrier usually adjusts his course and the tackle's head slides in front of the direction of the ball carrier. One of the worst mistakes the tackler can make is to drop his head. Not only does he loose sight of the ball carrier, but he is not susceptible to a head or neck injury. An intelligent tackler should work throughout the year to build up his neck and always use a bull neck technique when tackling.

On a sideline tackle, the tackler is taught to shoot his head in front of the ball carrier, popping the ball out of the runner's arms with a quick solid jolt. The tackler should step with the same foot, same shoulder, and this technique really makes a tackle "pop!" The tackler must use a solid base by keeping his feet well under his body (under the armpits).

The defensive tackler is taught to explode through the ball carrier, driving his arms up and through the ball carrier like two uppercuts. The coach must teach the tackler to lift and drive the arms at the same time and keep driving the legs until the whistle blows.

DEFENSIVE TACKLING DRILLS

The following five tackling drills are used in whole or part in all of our full gear practice sessions. All of our tackling drills stress technique rather than trying to prove just how hard an individual can hit. Once we have found our hitters, we want to just keep them sharp by tackling within a three yard square, rather than proving how tough a defender is every day of practice.

One on One Tackling Drill (Group):

Objective: Run through the ball carrier and drive him into the ground.

Organization: One ball carrier, one tackler. (Can be run by the numbers in a group.)

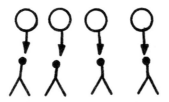

TACKLING DRILL (ONE ON ONE)
Diagram 7-58

Execution: The tackler should set his eyes on the ball carrier's target (bottom of the ball carrier's numbers). He should break down in a good football position, with his elbows in and his feet under his body. The head should be up and aimed directly for the bottom of the ball carrier's numbers. The eyes should be opened and focused on the target. The feet should accelerate at the moment of contact. The tackler should explode through the ball carrier without lowering or turning his body. He should explode up and through the ball carrier, wrapping the arms around the opponent. The legs should remain accelerating until the ball carrier is on his back. The ball carrier's head should be pointed toward his own goal line.

Coaching Points: Emphasize the contact and follow through tackling phase (Diagram 7-58).

Head to Head Tackling Drill:

Objective: Quick reaction from a critical position and make the tackle.

Organization: Two players lying down helmet to helmet, in opposite directions. Six air dummies should be set down three yards apart, on each side, to confine the ball carrier's area. One football is needed. A line is drawn two yards past the defender, simulating the goal line.

HEAD TO HEAD DRILL

Diagram 7-59

Execution: Coach hands either player the ball, and the ball carrier attempts to run past the defender. The defender is the player who does not have the ball when the coach yells, "Go!" Defender makes the tackle using any tackling technique he can master in this quick reaction drill.

Coaching Points: Tackler must get head in front and wrap his arms around the ball carrier. Don't let the ball carrier cross the goal line (Diagram 7-59).

Gang Tackling Circle Drill:

Objective: Teach gang tackling in close area.

Organization: Eight defenders form a circle with a ball carrier in the center.

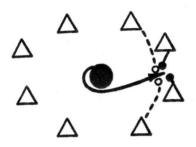

GANG TACKLING CIRCLE DRILL
Diagram 7-60

Execution: The ball carrier spins in a three hundred and sixty degree circle and attacks any gap of his choosing. As soon as the ball carrier attacks the gap, both defenders on each side of the gap tackle the ball carrier, with the next closest defenders joining in on the gang tackle. All defenders try to get a piece of the ball carrier before the coach blows the whistle.

Coaching Points: Once the ball carrier is stopped, the third and fourth defenders are coached to force the ball carrier to fumble. This technique is taught by pulling the ball out of the runner's arms, pulling away the ball carrying arm, or popping the ball loose with the helmet (Diagram 7-60).

Jolt Drill (Tackling):

Objective: Exploding placing helmet into target area. Important first phase in tackling.

Organization: Three defenders line up in a straight, parallel line. Opposite this line is an offensive ball carrier two yards away.

Execution: On "ready" command, three defenders begin to chop their feet. On "go" command, the offensive ball carrier attempts to lunge between two of the defenders. The defenders explode into the ball carrier, hitting him with their foreheads just at the base of the ball carrier's numbers. The offensive lunge and the explosion by the defenders often

JOLT DRILL (TACKLING)

Diagram 7-61

lift the ball carrier off his feet (four to five heet high) and push him back on his feet about two yards back. The defenders reset their line, and the ball carrier again attacks one of the gap areas. The offensive ball carrier takes four lunges at the defenders before changing personnel.

Coaching Points: Defenders must throw or rotate the hips on the defensive explosion. The defender's arms should be thrust forward on both sides of the ball carrier's hips (Diagram 7-61).

Defending the Score Drill:

Objective: Defense challenges the offense two on two.

Organization: Two dummies are set up to keep the two offensive and defensive players within a five yard area. Offensive blocker lines up two yards away from defensive linemen. Goal line is drawn one yard behind defenders.

DEFENDING THE SCORE DRILL

Diagram 7-62

Execution: Defenders move on blocker's movement and attack the offensive ball carrier. Defenders have backs to the goal line and must prevent the score. Both defenders must step up and go after the ball carrier with their shoulders parallel to the line of scrimmage. A poor tackle will result in a score for the offense.

Coaching Points: The defenders must be coached to move on movement and attack the ball carrier. Encourage gang tackling fundamentals (Diagram 7-62).

COACHING THE OUTSIDE LINEBACKERS "65"—"66"

Alignment: The outside linebacker should split the inside foot of the offensive end with the middle of his body in a "65" alignment. If there is a close wing back, he should line up head up on the offensive end in a "6" alignment to the split end's side (Diagrams 7-63 and 7-64).

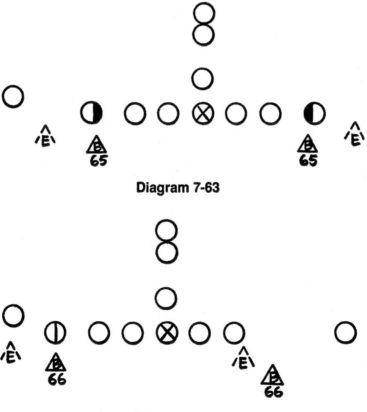

Diagram 7-63

Diagram 7-64

Stance: Two point stance with the back foot back. Keep shoulders parallel to the line of scrimmage. Hide the outside foot.

Coaching Point: Move on the defender's movement with a short jab step. Deliver a blow, same foot, same arm. Fight the pressure of the offensive end's block and fight through his head. Take the correct pursuit course. Never let the end release to your inside.

Key: Key the end. If knocked down or stacked, key the tackle.

Adjustments:

1. Regular
2. Split end—Knock down, read tackle
3. Stack—Read tackle

Reaction:

1. If run, attack the off-tackle hole from outside-in angle. If sweep, attack from inside-out angle. When pass shows, play coverage call. Hold and read if in doubt.
2. Straight drop back pass, normally sprint to assigned flat area (if no deep secondary defender is assigned the flat).
3. If play action shows and in doubt, pass or run—attack the ball.
4. If bootleg or sprint out shows, go to flat and attack passer only when he crosses line of scrimmage.

SPLIT, WEAK, OR SHORT SIDE ADJUSTMENTS

The short or weakside linebacker's specific alignment and assignment depends upon the signal caller's call. Against the tight end, the linebacker lines up in a "66" or "67" alignment and uses the "66" or "67" technique. The split side linebacker may also be assigned an (R) revert position, (F) force position, (S) stacked position, or (W) walk-away position.

Revert Position ("44" Technique): The revert shortside linebacker is coached to line head up on the weak or shortside tackle about two feet deeper than the heels of the defensive tackle ("44" technique). The linebacker should use his two point football stance with his shoulders squared away to the line of scrimmage (Diagram 7-65).

The weak or shortside linebacker's main responsibility is to close off the off-tackle play. He is coached to remain near the line of scrimmage, holding his position, to: first, fill inside of the defensive end's position;

Diagram 7-65

second, he is taught to help support to the outside on a wide sweep or quick pitch. He is coached to key the offensive tackle.

If flow goes away, the weak or shortside linebacker is coached to hold to determine whether the ball is going. If the opposition runs the ball up the middle, the linebacker is taught to attack the play from the inside out by squeezing the ball carrier. As soon as the ball goes away, the revert linebacker should look for a quick counter play or trap to the inside. If the ball continues to move away from his position, like a sweep or sprint out away, the weakside linebacker is coached to cushion or drop backward and then get into the proper pursuit pattern. He must continually look for bootleg and counter plays.

When a straight drop back pass develops, the linebacker should drop back into his hook area and look for a flare or divide pattern by the halfback. If no man is in his hook area, he should then drift into the outside one-sixth curl area and look for the curl pass. If no man enters the curl area, he should continue to drop backward so that he never becomes a useless pass defender covering only space or an empty defensive pass zone.

Force Position ("67" Technique) (Diagram 7-66): The force position is a position about one yard outside of the defensive end and on the

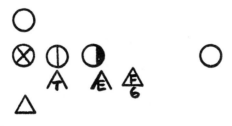

Diagram 7-66

line of scrimmage (''67'' technique). He is coached to use a two point stance, with the shoulders parallel to the goal line, and the inside foot should be slightly ahead of the outside foot.

The force defender is taught to key the frontside halfback, and he is responsible to contain all outside plays. On the snap of the ball, the force linebacker is coached to take a quick, short step forward with the inside foot, and then shuffle the outside leg forward so that both the feet and the shoulders are parallel to the goal line.

The force linebacker is responsible to force and contain all plays his way. If the ball carrier cuts up inside of his position, he must be sure to check for a quick cut to the outside. As soon as he is sure he has contained all outside threats, he is then coached to attack off-tackle or play up the middle from an outside-in angle.

If a sweep or sprint out develops away from the force man, he is taught that he must cushion backward and look for a possible throw back pass. If there is no throw back threat, the force linebacker is coached to get into his correct pursuit course.

When the quarterback uses a quick drop back pocket pass, the linebacker is coached to take the drop back in the hook area first, and then slide to the outside one-sixth curl zone area.

If a sprint out pass develops toward the force linebacker, he is coached to attack the sprint out pass as long as one of the deep secondary defenders gives him an ''up'' call. This ''up'' call is given when one of the defenders has the flat area similar to a level or change (invert) defensive pass coverage call.

Stack Position (''445'' Technique): The shortside linebacker may adjust his position to a stacked position directly behind the defensive end (''445'' position). The linebacker is coached to use a two point football position (Diagram 7-67).

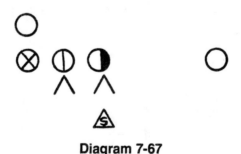

Diagram 7-67

The stack position is taught to key the defensive tackle and is responsible to stop the inside play first and the outside play second. The only difference in this assignment is when the defensive linebacker is called upon to stunt to the outside, and the defensive end fires into the inside. On this stunt, the end just assumes the stacked linebacker's normal inside assignment, while the linebacker assumes the defensive end's outside assignment.

Normally, the stacked linebacker uses the same technique as the revert linebacker (R position) (Diagram 7-65).

Walk-Away Position ("88" Technique): The walk-away linebacker uses a parallel football stance and lines up equidistant between the split receiver and the offensive tackle (Diagram 7-68).

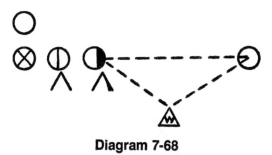

Diagram 7-68

The walk-away linebacker is responsible for the pass first and a run second. On a running play toward the "W" man, he has force-contain responsibility. If the ball goes away from the "W" position, the walk-away defender is coached to look for a throw back pass and then is taught to cushion backward and get into his correct pursuit pattern.

This position is an assignment that we use fewer and fewer times each year. The reason for this is that the walk-away position places the defender in a difficult inbetween position where he cannot focus his full attention on a run or a pass. Therefore, we usually place the linebacker closer to our defensive end to stop the opposition's run.

DOUBLE COVER ("9" TECHNIQUE)

The linebacker takes up an inside position or outside position on the split end so that he may be able to chug the split receiver as he drives off the line of scrimmage. The double covering linebacker may force the split end to the outside or funnel him in to the inside, depending upon the secondary pass coverage, down, distance, or favorite pass pattern by the split receiver (Diagram 7-69).

As soon as the linebacker collisions the split receiver, he is coached to drop back into the flat and check for the possibility of the near back running a flat or flare pass pattern into his area. If the split receiver goes deep and no one enters the flat area, the double covering linebacker is coached to continue to retreat deep so that he is not just "covering air" or space.

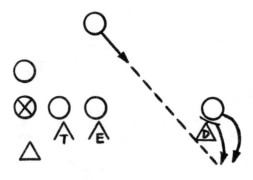

Diagram 7-69

If a sweep or option play comes his way, the linebacker holds his position until he is sure it is a run. As soon as he determines run, he attacks the wide play as a secondary contain man and tries to force or squeeze the wide play to the inside. If the play goes away, the linebacker drops back into the flat zone, looks for a throw back pass or delayed reverse, and then gets into his proper pursuit course.

When the quarterback sprints out his way, the double covering linebacker chugs the split receiver and plays his flat. The only time the double covering linebacker attacks the sprint out quarterback is when the quarterback outruns the defensive end's containment. When this play takes place, the linebacker is coached to force contain the quarterback and is coached to squeeze the runner to the inside, so that the defensive pursuit is able to attack the quarterback.

PASS COVERAGE RESPONSIBILITY FOR WEAK LINEBACKER

The weak or shortside linebacker, to the split end's side in a normal, revert, force, or stacked position, is coached to drop back into his hook zone versus a straight drop back pass. As soon as he begins his drop, the linebacker should look up the near halfback and collision him if the halfback attempts to run a divide pass pattern into the deep seam between the split end and the offensive tackle (Diagram 7-70).

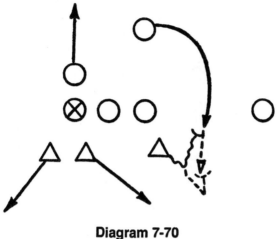

Diagram 7-70

If the offensive halfback runs a flat or flare route, the outside linebacker is coached to pick up the halfback and maintain a three yard cushion on this potential receiver (Diagram 7-71).

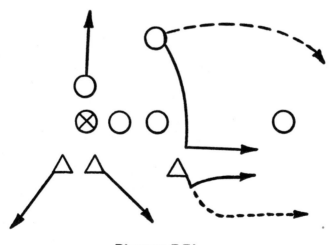

Diagram 7-71

If the offensive halfback blocks, the linebacker is taught to sprint back into the curl zone and look for the split end on his curl pattern. The curl area is the outside one-sixth zone, and the linebacker should drop back about ten yards deep (Diagram 7-72). His target area should be the apex of the triangle formed by the offensive tackle and the split end (Diagram 7-73).

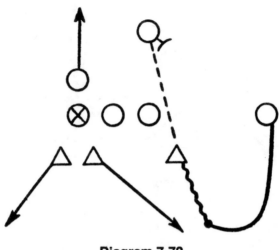

Diagram 7-72

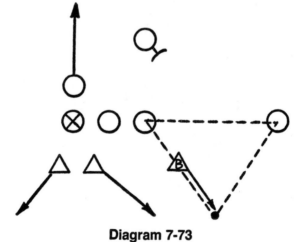

Diagram 7-73

Generally, the short or weakside linebacker is responsible for secondary contain on a sweep or wide maneuver, and goes to the hook zone on a straight drop back pass. If flow goes away, the shortside linebacker is coached to open up away from the flow and check for the crossing or delayed tight end or the halfback running some type of a flare, flat, or seam pass pattern. On all drop back passes with the halfback running a divide pass pattern into the seam, the shortside linebacker has the halfback all the way.

The weakside linebacker is coached to call all screen passes and to react to these screens quickly. He must watch the quarterback's feet and set up as soon as the passer sets up and then quickly react to the quarterback's pass. Always hold for the play action pass. The shortside linebacker is responsible to play run first and then pass second. The shortside linebacker is responsible to make sure that the alignment of all linemen to his side is correct. He also adjusts his own alignment and depth depending upon scouting reports, film breakdowns, and down and distance information.

SPREAD COVERAGE ADJUSTMENT (SPLIT 40 DEFENSE)

Cornerman—Never be flanked by one man.

Outside Linebacker—Never be flanked by two men (Diagram 7-74).

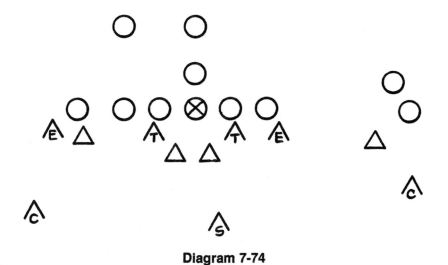

Diagram 7-74

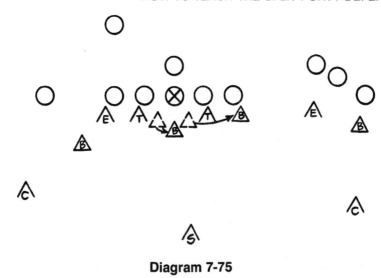

Diagram 7-75

End—Never be flanked by three men (Diagram 7-75).

We use these spread rules to take care of any unorthodox offensive spread formations the opposition may use against us. We attach the code name, "garbage," to these spread formations because we tell our defensive players that the opposition depends upon "garbage" to beat us with these spread defenses. This psychological approach to shotgun or spread formation gives the defense the necessary poise and confidence to defend against these wide sets.

OUTSIDE LINEBACKER DRILLS (SPLIT FORTY DEFENSE)

We use the same Outside Linebacker Drills for the Split Forty Defense as we do in the Forty Defense Outside Linebacker Drills. (See Chapter Four, Drills—Diagrams 4-28, 4-29, 4-30.)

The Linebacker Fight the Pressure Drill (Diagram 7-76) and the Linebacker Expansion Drill (Diagram 7-77) can be used by both the Split 40 and the 40 Defenses. The Rope Drills (Diagram 7-78, 7-79, 7-80, and 7-81) cannot only be used by the outside linebackers in the Split 40 Defense, but by all defenders regardless of the defense used. The Rope Drills are excellent teaching devices to help develop quick feet, balance, and agility.

Linebacker Fight Pressure Drill:

Objective: Put defender in the critical position (blocked), and then make

LINEBACKER FIGHT PRESSURE DRILL

Diagram 7-76

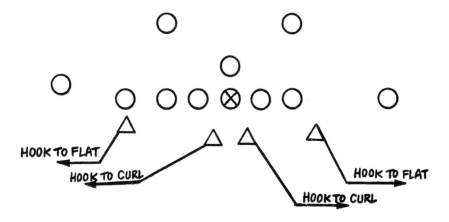

HOOK TO FLAT

HOOK TO CURL

HOOK TO FLAT

HOOK TO CURL

LINEBACKER EXPANSION DRILL

Diagram 7-77

the defender fight through the head of the blocker and cut off the ball carrier (fight pressure).

Organization: Put the blocker in the perfect blocking position and the defender in the critical (blocked) position. Ball carrier, blocker, and defender are used in this drill.

Execution: Teach defender how to fight out of the critical position by fighting the offensive blocker's pressure (through the blocker's head). Coach signals ball carrier to move one side or the other and coaches the

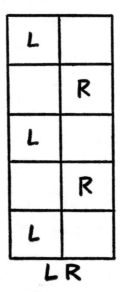

RUN ALTERNATE SQUARES

Diagram 7-78

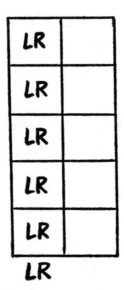

HOP TO ONE SIDE

Diagram 7-79

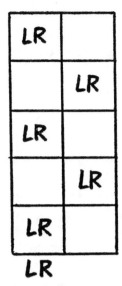

LR

HOP ALTERNATE SQUARES

Diagram 7-80

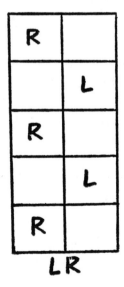

LR

RUN CROSSOVER STEPS

Diagram 7-81

defender the proper method to defeat the blocker and attack the ball carrier (Diagram 7-76).

Coaching Points: Go through the blocker's head. Use the hands to get rid of a low scramble blocker (Diagram 7-76).

Linebacker's Expansion Drill:

Objective: Teach linebackers to cover their zones and to expand if no one enters their zone.

Organization: Four defensive linebackers in their respective positions and at least three potential receivers.

Execution: Linebackers drop back to their respective zones. Straight drop back pass—inside linebackers protect hook zone; then, expand to curl zones if no one is in their zones. Outside linebackers drop to flat to formation side and hook to flat to the short side of the offensive formation.

Coaching Points: Teach all four linebackers to key, read on the move, and expand their zones (Diagram 7-77).

The Rope Drills:

Objective: Develop quick feet, balance, and agility.

Organization: Two rows of parallel ropes, squares, or tires.

Execution: The player runs the ropes or tires by starting with his left foot in the first left square and then alternates squares or tires with alternate feet (Diagram 7-78—Run Alternate Squares).

The player hops through two feet at a time up the left side (Diagram 7-79—Hop One Side).

The player hops into alternate areas two feet at a time (Diagram 7-80—Hop Alternate Squares).

The player runs through the line using cross over steps alternately (Diagram 7-81—Run Cross Over Steps).

Coaching Points: Emphasize twisting hips and develop pride in quick feet, hitting the center of each area.

Chapter 8

Coaching Forty Over
and Under Defense

An alternate defense to the basic Split Forty and Forty Defenses is the Forty Over and Under adjustments. Using the over and under calls, we are able to give the offense an odd look (man on the line of scrimmage over the center in an "0" technique).

The defensive signal caller calls the adjustment in the defensive huddle. The defensive line slides to the over or under call, once the offensive team has lined up on the line of scrimmage and has indicated the offensive formation set. The side of the stunt is called, after the defense has shuffled over or under, with a "Lucky" call indicating the left side will go through with the stunt and a "Ringo" call indicating the right side will go through with the predetermined stunt. The defensive signal caller is encouraged to call some false "Lucky" and "Ringo" calls when we are in our normal or regular over or under call, to keep the opposition "honest."

Our linebackers are coached to move around near their assigned areas in order to hide their defensive intentions, but the linebackers must be able to arrive at their assigned area when the ball is snapped. In specific games, the nose tackle uses various techniques and methods of disguising his defensive intentions whenever he is not called into the defensive stunt. He may also move back off the line of scrimmage a couple of yards. Whether on or off the line of scrimmage, the nose defender may use one of the following techniques: offset and go, offset and fire back into the center, step around, play hard-nosed, or play it soft and flow to the ball.

FORTY OVER AND UNDER CALLS

When we use a Forty Over or a Forty Under call, we want to give the offense an odd look. An odd look moves one of our defensive tackle's head up and close to the offensive center. This odd look also places our two big strong tackles close to each other, giving the offensive quarterback a different picture of our defense.

The word "over" against a balanced offensive line with two tight ends means "right" to the defense (Diagram 8-1). The word "under" against a balanced offensive line with two tight ends means "left" to our defense (Diagram 8-2).

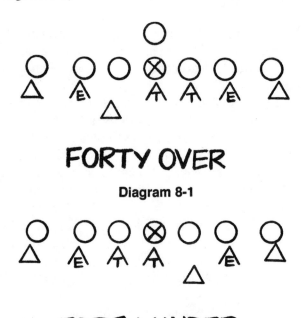

FORTY OVER

Diagram 8-1

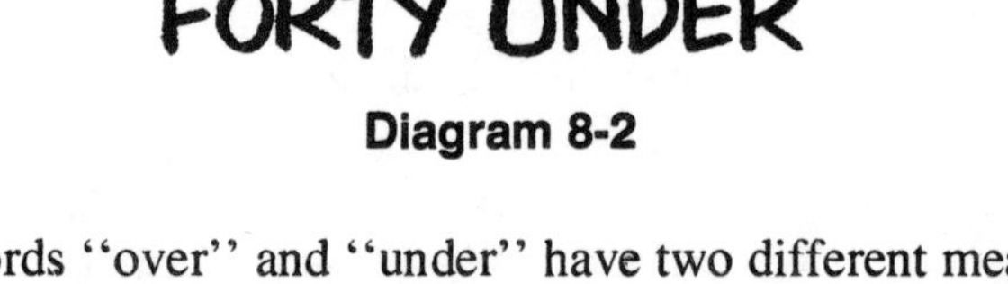

FORTY UNDER

Diagram 8-2

The words "over" and "under" have two different meanings if the offense employs a split end formation. With a split end, the defensive word "over" means toward the tight end or the strong side of the formation. The word "under" means to the split end or the weak side of the formation. Forty Over versus a split end to the defense's right is illustrated in Diagram 8-3. Forty Over versus a split end to the defense's left is

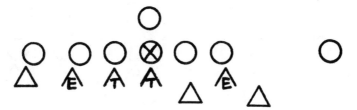

FORTY OVER

Diagram 8-3

pictured in Diagram 8-4. Diagram 8-5 shows Forty Under against a split end to the defense's right, while Diagram 8-6 illustrates the Forty Under call versus a split end to the defense's left.

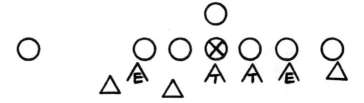

FORTY OVER

Diagram 8-4

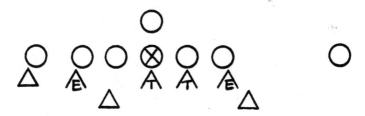

FORTY UNDER

Diagram 8-5

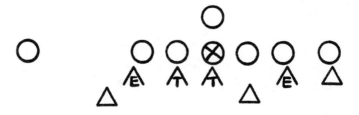

FORTY UNDER

Diagram 8-6

DEFENSIVE END AND LINEBACKER PLAY "67"

Since both the defensive end and outside linebackers play the "67" defensive position, he should be specifically called the "67" defender; but, since it is basically the end man on the line of scrimmage, I have referred to him as the defensive end in this defensive explanation.

Position and Alignment

The defensive end lines up splitting the offensive end's outside foot. At times the depth and the position of alignment may change depending upon the assigned defense, down and distance. The width of the defensive end's position is dictated by the stunt called by our defensive signal caller.

Stance

The end ("67") lines up in a two point stance keeping his outside foot back so that the blocker will be unable to hook him in. The feet should be in a comfortable position, about as wide as the armpits. He should be in a football position ready to attack from the time the offensive team leaves the huddle. The offensive end's helmet is his first key. He should look through the helmet into the enemy's backfield.

Responsibilities

We ask the defensive end to perform more assignments than any other defender. To carry out all of these multi-responsibilities, he must be agile, hard-nosed, and quick.

He must help to keep the offensive end off the left defensive "44" man, using his forearm blow. He must stop the off-tackle play. The defensive end must also be able to contain the reverse, bootleg and counter plays. He must stop the sweep and never get hooked by the offensive end. In rushing the passer, he must attack from the outside in. The defender may also be called into our pass coverage plans. The end should employ a deep pursuit angle. At times he must set a course for the flag.

Charge

The end should explode on the first movement of the offensive end. The charge should be ignited with a short jab step with the inside foot directly into the offensive end. He must make solid contact with the inside forearm blow to the opposition's base of the neck. An alternate method of contact is to use both hands. Smash the inside hand to the opponent's forehead forcing his head back, while the outside hand should smash his shoulder, forcing him backward and to the inside. He should keep the thumbs in. As soon as he makes contact, he must drive at the opponent with fast, short and choppy steps. The defender should maintain balance while he controls the blocker, allowing for a quick release to attack the ball carrier.

He must fight pressure through the head of the blocker and drive him back and in. If the offensive end goes to the outside to hook the defender, he should meet the blocker and fight to the outside, using his arms to keep the blocker away from his feet. If the blocker starts to take the end in, the defender should pivot back and around to the outside. The defensive end should never let the end release without delivering a blow. He should knock him off stride, step down to the inside to help close the off-tackle hole.

The offensive back to the defender's side may try to block him in or out. The "67" man should look for a block from the inside by a trapping guard, tackle, or fullback. If blocked, the defender should attack from the inside, meet the blocker with the outside foot back and anchored. He should keep the body low and deliver a blow with the inside foot (same arm, same foot), attempting to stop the blocker with a strong forearm. The defensive end should attack the blocker, keeping the shoulders parallel to the line of scrimmage. If the power sweep develops, he must shuffle to the outside, forcing the sweep deep and to the outside. He should not penetrate more than a yard and one-half beyond the line of scrimmage unless rushing the passer.

If the back attempts to use the hook block, the defensive end should meet him with a forearm aimed at his chest, keeping his feet free. He must not go around the blocker; always fight through his head. A good defender always uses his hands. He should play the blocker first and then stop the ball carrier.

Pursuit

If the ball carrier goes to the other side of the center, the end should hold and look for a reverse, counter or bootleg. Then the defender should begin to pursue intelligently to head off the runner. He must never turn his back to the ball.

Punt Rush

A defender can only block a punt by getting into the kicking lane. He must set his sights on the point where the kicker will actually kick. Then he should go all out for that point. It takes courage to block a kick.

Pass Rush

As soon as the rusher sees a pocket pass developing, rush the passer from the outside in. Expect the passer to attempt to scramble out of his pocket. The defensive end should holler "Pass" as soon as he recognizes a pass developing. Always rush with the arms high, forcing the passer to throw with a high trajectory. This affords the secondary a better chance for an interception.

As the passer cocks his arm to throw, the rusher should tackle him from the top down. He must try to pin his arms to his sides. The second rusher should go for the ball. As soon as the passer releases the ball, the defender must peel off to the side of the ball to be in position to block in case of an interception.

When rushing, the defender should key the back to his side because he may release for a screen or flare pass. If the passer drops back more than seven yards deep, the defender must read screen.

Playing the Walk-Away Position

Any time the offensive end is removed or split more than four yards, the defender may be assigned to drop off the line of scrimmage and split the distance between the split end and the offensive tackle. At the last moment he may wish to move back into his forcing position.

The defender must attack all sweeps from the outside in. On roll outs he should attack the quarterback. On roll outs away, he must drop back and cover the flat and continue into his revolve patterns. On drop back or pocket passes, he should cover the flat. The "67" defender must support the off-tackle plays to his side from the outside in.

If there is a slot to his side, he should use the slot rule. The defender's key is then near back and the ball.

DEFENSIVE TACKLE AND END PLAY "45"

Alignment and Position

The defensive tackle must line up splitting the offensive tackle's outside foot. If the offensive tackle takes an abnormally large split, he should move quickly to his inside just prior to the snap of the ball. Then he should shoot the inside gap and set his sights for the ball carrier.

Stance

He should take a four point defensive stance. He must stay as low as possible keeping his feet under him so that he can quickly spring into action. The "45" man must line up in a parallel stance with a heel and toe relationship. His feet should be tucked up under him about the width of his armpits.

The end should focus his eyes on the offensive tackle's helmet and into the backfield. His hands should be placed about one and one-half feet in front of his forward foot. The "45" defender's elbows must be slightly outside of his knees, with his head and shoulders as low as possible.

Responsibilities

Approximately 80 percent of all of football's running plays are directed at the off-tackle area. The tackle must be a strong anchor. He must play his area first. If his area is not under attack, he must shoot into the running lane low and in his prescribed manner. He must never be taken in or hooked by the offensive tackle. He must keep the offensive tackle off the linebacker by using his forearm blow. The tackle should check for the screen pass to his side whenever he is not blocked. The rusher should think "screen" whenever the passer drops back deeper than usual.

Keys

If the head of the offensive tackle goes to the inside, he should shuffle to the inside. When the tackle's head goes to the outside, the defender must make sure he is not hooked and should step to his outside, keeping the inside arm free. If he has trouble reading his keys, he must move slightly off the line of scrimmage.

Charge and Pursuit

All defenders must be ready to explode as soon as the center touches the ball. They should move on movement, reacting to beat their opponent's charge and take the initiative away from the offensive blocker.

The defensive tackle should take a short six inch step with his front or inside foot and deliver a forearm blow (same foot, same arm). The target for his forearm should be just below the offensive tackle's shoulder as he drives out in his three point offensive stance.

The defender must stay low, and at contact take a short step with the outside foot, keeping his shoulders squared to the goal line. The one and one-half shuffle step must be quick. Continual practice will help the defender master this important defensive technique. He must use his free arm to fight his opponent and quickly get rid of him. The tackle should avoid wrestling with him. The blocker should never tie up the defender's feet.

Follow through with a short choppy step to help reach his assigned point. The tackle must strive to reach his point on each play. When he reaches his point, he should be low and squared away. The "45" man must not penetrate deeper than one yard, except on a pass play. The defensive axiom is "minimum penetration and maximum pursuit." On plays to his outside, he must fight pressure to get outside. If he is double teamed, he must spin out to the outside and take the proper pursuit course to intercept the play.

On plays away, he should cross the line of scrimmage and trail. As soon as the ball crosses the line of scrimmage, he must take his proper pursuit angle. He must trail so he can break up any counters, reverses, or bootlegs that may come back his way. The "45" defender is taught to fight pressure going through the head of the blocker. The tackle must be prepared to spin out if he feels himself being blocked. If he does not feel any resistance by the time he has reached his point, he must begin to shuffle to the inside, expecting a trap. The four point defender must keep his shoulders parallel to the line of scrimmage. Only after he has determined that he is not under attack, should he trail. Remember the defender may use his hands on defense.

The defender should never spread more than fingertip to fingertip, man to man, when the arms of the defense are spread. The only change in this philosophy will be pre-arranged. If the opposition leaves a gap, he should be ready to shoot into this gap and power into the backfield. If the defender can't make the gap, he must take away the offensive blocking angle when the defensive tackle delivers a blow. The defender must be set to charge into the man who has flanked him and react to the offensive maneuver.

Pass Rush

Key for draws and screens. A key for a screen is when the quarterback drops back further than his usual six yard drop back position. The tackle should key draw by focusing his eyes upon the near back and as the quarterback passes by, he may give the ball to the running back.

If the end is rushing, he should rush from the outside in so the defensive tackle can help protect the middle on a draw or a quarterback scramble up the middle. If the end is assigned the flat zone, the tackle to that side must rush from the outside in so that he can contain the passer. As soon as the passer throws the ball, the tackle must peel off to his side so he will be in position to block for an interception.

Punt Rush

The defender should aim at a point just in front of where the kicker will actually make his kick. He must get into the kicking lane quickly if he expects to block a kick. Only hard-nosed defenders block kicks.

DEFENSIVE LINEBACKER PLAY "223"

Alignment and Position

The defensive linebacker should line up splitting the offensive guard's outside foot. Generally his depth will be slightly deeper than the heels of the nose tackle.

He should crowd the guard on short yardage situations. Usually he will loosen up on long yardage situations depending upon the defensive game stragety. If the defensive guard's split is abnormal, the linebacker should be prepared to shoot the gap between the center and the guard. With an abnormal split we advise the linebacker to line up on his regular alignment and then move up and in just prior to the snap of the ball.

Stance

The linebacker should use a parallel two point stance which will enable him to move quickly in any direction. We call this the "ready" or football position. The feet should be placed in a comfortable position. Arms should be "hands" down to protect his feet. We want the linebacker to stay low; therefore, his arms will be lower to better protect his legs. If the guard pulls in either direction, we want him to scallop in the direction, keeping his shoulders parallel to the line of scrimmage. Scalloping is a fast shuffling action. The weight should be placed on the balls of the feet and his eyes should be fixed on the offensive guard's helmet. On the snap of the ball, he should take a set step, then react to his key. Next he should pick out the ball carrier and pursue him, getting into his running lane.

Responsibilities

The linebacker's area of responsibility is from the head of the offensive guard to the head of his near offensive tackle. He should never let the guard hook him or take him inside. He must play the run first and the pass second. The linebacker is coached to scallop in the direction of the guard's pulling direction. He must be able to support any area from sideline to sideline.

A linebacker must never get knocked off his feet. He should move as his key moves, deliver a blow, and then get to the point of attack. The linebacker must meet the ball carrier with his shoulders parallel to the goal line. He should deliver a blow on the offensive guard and then get rid of him as soon as possible. He should not make it a private war between himself and the offensive guard. He must get rid of the blocker quickly and then pursue.

Example of Responsibility

If the offensive guard blocks out on him, he must deliver a blow and fight his blocking pressure, working toward the inside. On any sweep or off-tackle play to his outside, he should not let the offensive guard hook him or take him to the inside. The defender must play through the head of the blocker, get rid of him, and get into the running lane. He should go in the same direction as the pulling guard. On all drop back passes he should yell "Pass," then he must sprint back into his hook or curl zone.

Charge and Pursuit

The linebacker should be coached to take a set step into the blocker and deliver a forearm blow into the offensive man's chest. If the guard blocks him, he should deliver a blow with his inside arm, using the outside hand to control and get rid of the blocking guard. Keeping his shoulders below the blocker's shoulders, he should use his defensive blow to neutralize the blocker. Next, he must locate the ball and pursue the ball carrier.

The linebacker should mirror the offensive guard because he is his key. When scalloping laterally in pursuit of the ball carrier, he must make sure he does not overrun the ball carrier. He must make sure he is just a step behind the ball carrier so that he cannot only stop the cutback, but he may also take a deeper pursuit angle to head off the runner. He should scallop close to the line of scrimmage so that he just clears the line blocking areas.

The first step should be taken with the foot to the side he is going. He should never overrun the ball carrier. Once the ball is ready to be put into play and until the whistle blows, he must be ready to hit.

When the flow is away from him, he should check counter or reverse, then go through the other linebacker's position on his pursuit course. He must make sure he takes a deep enough angle to cut off the ball carrier. The linebacker should never overestimate his speed.

DEFENSIVE NOSE TACKLE PLAY "0"

Position and Alignment

The defensive nose tackle should line up head on the offensive center. At times his depth and alignment will be determined by the defensive call. Basically he will be two feet from the ball. The nose tackle may wish to crowd the center on short yardage situations. He must make sure he plays tight enough so that he can deliver a quick solid blow into the center. The defender should loosen slightly when he is involved in a stunt. He should play off the line on long yardage situations. Offset, stack and gap alignments and assignments will be assigned to him by the defensive signal caller.

Stance

The nose tackle should use a four point parallel stance. The feet should only be the width of his armpits. The head and eyes should be directly on the ball, as he is the only defender whose starting key is the ball. His elbows should be slightly outside of his knees. The hands should be placed on the ground about one and one-half feet in front of his up foot.

Responsibilities

The nose tackle should direct his responsibility from the nose of the offensive right guard to the nose of the left guard. He should be ready to react to the blocks of the center and both guards. He must check for offensive draws and screens. If he is sure no screen or draw exists, then he must rush the passer. If the play is not directed toward the center, he must pursue the ball.

Variations of Charge

He should continually confuse the center by varying his defensive charges. At times he should vary his alignment. Techniques to be used:

1. Blast—Sell out. All-out forearm blows should be aimed at the center's neck. He must use his other hand to control the center, as he must be able to go to either side.

2. Jam—The nose tackle should use this technique in long yardage situations after he has loosened. The defender should use a forearm blow by jamming the center's head into the ground. He should keep the blocker away from his feet, then locate the ball and pursue.

3. Step Around—

a. First he must take a jab step in the proper direction with the frontside foot.

b. Next, he should use his hands to push the center's head and shoulder away from his body.

c. The defender must whip the back leg around, sliding it behind the center's original position.

d. He must keep his shoulders parallel to the line of scrimmage.

e. If the play goes away, he should take a flat pursuit course and pursue the ball.

f. If the play is directed toward his area, he should destroy the ball carrier.

4. Stunt Called—The nose tackle should disregard caution and blast into his assigned area. He must get into the running lane and pile up the play.

Pass Rush

He is responsible first for the middle screen and draw. He is a secondary rusher. The nose man should yell "Pass!" if a pass develops. All defenders are taught to tackle the passer from the top down. The second man to hit the passer should go for the ball. The "0" man must peel off to the side of the pass in the event of an interception. As he rushes, he should check the fullback for the ball on a draw maneuver.

Punt Rush

A punt can only be blocked by the defender if he gets into the kicking lane. The target to block the punt is two yards in front of the punter. It takes a *man* to block a punt.

DEFENSIVE CORNERBACK PLAY

Stance

The cornerback's stance should be an upright football position. He is taught to use two point stance in a balanced position, knees bent, arms hanging loosely, eyes on your key, and shoulders parallel to the line of scrimmage. His outside foot should be back.

Steps

If he is in a zone pass defense and a pass shows, he must take a set step and read his keys. Then, sprint to his assigned area. If a run shows his way, the defender has force-contained responsibilities. If the ball goes away, he must take proper pursuit angle.

Man to man secondary call designates the defender to key his assigned man and react.

Keys (Zone)

He is coached to key the end and the closest back to his side. If the end blocks in, he must come up keying the back. If the end goes across field and the nearest back goes away, he must get into his revolve pattern. If the end releases, he should key the quarterback and sprint to his area of responsibility.

His other key is the ball. The cornerback should locate the ball and keep his eyes on it. He should maintain the same relationship with the ball that he had when he reached the center of his area.

Responsibilities

If the sweep comes his way, he should use his corner force-contain method of stopping the sweep. He should not gain his depth and wait for the ball. He should move toward the ball carrier, forcing him to cut the sweep up to the inside. The most important job on the sweep is to *contain*. Therefore, he should not wait as he opens up too large a hole between the defensive end and cornerback. He should keep an approximate three yard parallel relationship with his defensive end. He must keep his shoulders parallel to the line of scrimmage. The cornerback must meet force with his inside foot forward. He should keep the blockers away from his feet with his hands. The cornerback should never get knocked off his feet. He should be smart and fake the blocker into throwing his block too soon or off balance.

If the sweep develops away, the cornerback must check for counters, reverses and bootlegs. Next, he should get into his revolve pattern. He must be ready for some type of a cutback or a runner reversing his field and coming back into his area. If a sprint out play goes away, he should be ready for the quarterback's throw back or cross country pass.

If a drop back pass shows, he must drop back into the middle of his assigned zone. The defender must go for the ball directly through the receiver.

DEFENSIVE SAFETYMAN PLAY

Stance

The stance should be a well-balanced football position. This is a two point stance with his shoulders parallel to the line of scrimmage. He should start out with a parallel stance but some defenders prefer to drop their outside foot back, using a slightly staggered stance.

Steps

If pass shows and he is in a zone assignment, he should take a step back with the outside foot and take a picture of the play. The safetyman should key and sprint to his assigned zone and level off in the middle of that zone. If a run shows, he must take the proper pursuit course to reach the ball carrier.

Keys

The safety should key the offensive "end's area" (end, end and wing, end and slot). If the "end's area" blocks him to the inside, he must locate the ball and support. His general course on sweeps his way is to support outside of the cornerback. (If he tries to support the sweep his way, inside of the cornerback, the ball carrier may go all the way if the cornerman is knocked down). If the "end's area" releases crossfield, he must check for counters, reverses, or bootleg plays. If no action his way, he is coached to get into the revolve pattern.

Responsibilities

When the sweep goes his way, he should be ready to support the sweep to the outside of the cornerman. If the ball carrier cuts back to the inside, the safety must attack the ball carrier from the oustide in. The ball carrier's cutback will bring him into the pursuing defenders.

If the sweep goes away, the safety should check the counters, reverses, and bootlegs. He must get into the revolve pattern only after the ball carrier has crossed the line of scrimmage. He should watch for the cutback play. He must not get knocked off his feet. He must use his hands to keep blockers away from his body. He may give ground, but shouldn't let the blocker tangle him up. The safetyman should give ground and take the proper pursuit angle. When pass shows, he must cover his area or man. The deep defender must keep his eyes on the ball. A good defensive man continually talks it up. He should repeat his responsibilities and remind his teammates of their assignments.

Tackle Box

This is an area in the offensive backfield between the offensive outside shoulder of the offensive tackles.

If the passer stays inside this area, it is considered a drop back pass. If the passer sprints outside this imaginary area, it is considered a sprint out pass. When the passer sprints outside this area the safetyman should yell, "Sprint out!"

Chapter 9

Defensive Techniques for the Forty Over and Under Defenses

After we have written down the technical aspects of the defensive individual's position, alignments, stance, responsibilities, charge, pursuit, pass rush and punt rush, we feel it is necessary to diagram each individual's techniques, for both the coaching staff and defensive players.

Our coaching staff believes that one diagram takes the place of a hundred words. Therefore, we clearly diagram each technique that our defensive players may encounter. This has been an important reason for the success of our defense. Whenever a player sees and understands what he is supposed to do, he is able to carry out his assignment at game time.

DEFENSIVE TECHNIQUE FOR ENDS AND LINEBACKERS "67"

While it is either the defensive end or linebacker who is assigned to play the "67" technique and alignment, it is the defensive end who is referred to instead of the linebacker in the following techniques.

End Blocks In and Halfback Tries for Hook Block (Diagram 9-1):

The defensive end should not let the halfback get outside position. He must shuffle outside and use his hands to keep the blocker away from his legs. Play through the blocker's head and make the tackle. He may be forced to give ground to keep from being hooked.

End Blocks In and Torpedo Attack at You (Diagram 9-2):

He must deliver a blow on the end and close down. The defender

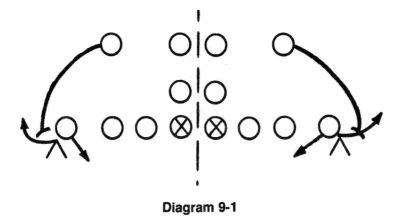

Diagram 9-1

should stay low and split the torpedo blockers, dipping his inside shoulder. The defensive end may have to go down to one knee—then react to the ball carrier.

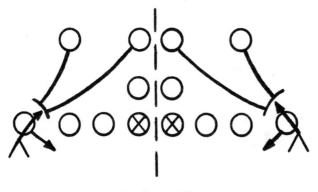

Diagram 9-2

End Blocks In and Back Blocks Out (Diagram 9-3):

The defender is coached to deliver a blow and step to the inside as the end blocks down. He must key the near back and deliver a forearm blow into the back with the inside arm. The defensive end must fight through the back's head and close down the off-tackle hole, staying low and ready for a quick dive off tackle.

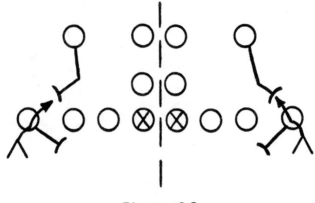

Diagram 9-3

End Blocks Down, Fullback Kicks Out (Diagram 9-4):

The "67" defender should close down if the end blocks down using the shuffle technique. First check the near back, then step into the fullback and deliver a blow with the inside arm. The defender should then fight through his head and close the off-tackle hole.

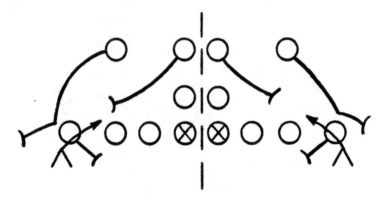

Diagram 9-4

Cross Block (Diagram 9-5):

If the offensive end blocks inside, the defender should shuffle inside and deliver a forearm blow into cross blocking tackle. The end must be lower than the blocking tackle.

End Blocks In and Guard Traps (Diagram 9-6):

The end is coached to deliver a blow on the end as he blocks in and

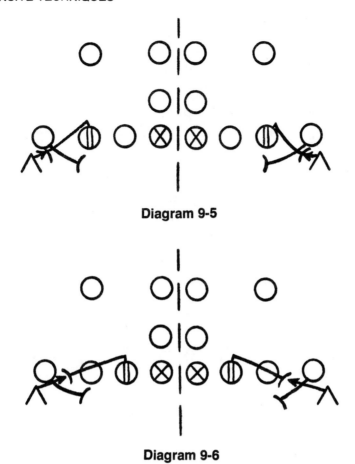

Diagram 9-5

Diagram 9-6

checks the near side back. Then, he must key the trapping guard, while shuffling to the inside and keeping his shoulders parallel to the line of scrimmage. The end must meet the trap man with his inside forearm, keeping his shoulders leveled off to the line. The "67" defender gains leverage on the trapper by staying lower than the trap man.

End Blocks Out (Diagram 9-7):

The end is taught to fight pressure through the head of the blocking end. He must close the off-tackle hole and get rid of the blocker as soon as possible. The end must next get into position to make the tackle.

End Tries to Hook Block (Diagram 9-8):

The defensive end must give ground if he has to, so he will not be

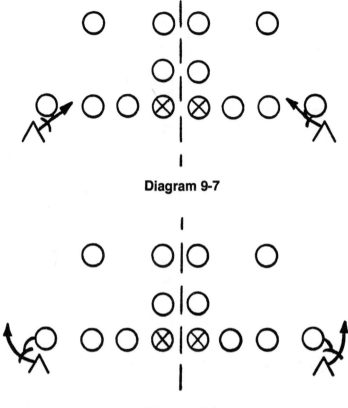

Diagram 9-7

Diagram 9-8

hooked. He must use his hands to keep the blocker away from his feet. He must look for the frontside back as soon as he gets rid of the end. Next, the defender should fight through the end's head to make the play.

End Releases, Back Tries to Hook You (Diagram 9-9):

The defender must deliver a blow on the releasing end and fight outside of the back's hook block; then, play through the back's block and be set to make the tackle.

Drop Back Pass (Diagram 9-10):

The defensive end's assignment is to deliver a blow on the offensive end and rush from the outside in on the drop back passer, unless he is in the defensive pass coverage call. The end must not let the passer scramble outside of him.

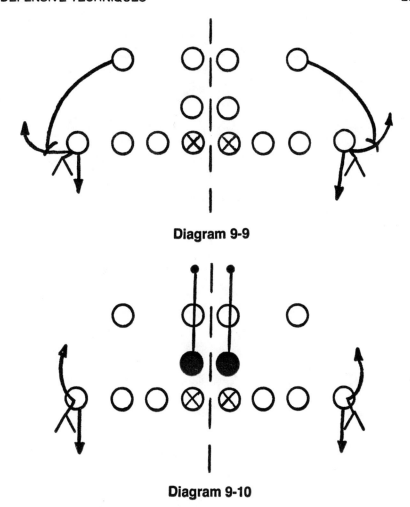

Diagram 9-9

Diagram 9-10

Sprint Out Pass–Away (Diagram-11):

If the defender is assigned the flat, he should cover the flat dropping off the line once he recognizes the pass. If assigned to rush, the defender must set a course directly at the passer and unload on him from the backside.

Sprint Out Pass–To (Diagram 9-12):

The defensive end must attack the passer if he sprints out to his side, regardless of the pass coverage. He must contain the sprint out by rushing from the outside in.

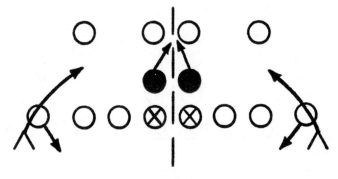

Diagram 9-11

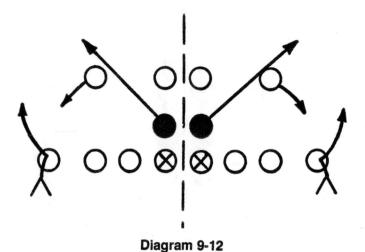

Diagram 9-12

DEFENSIVE LINEBACKER'S TECHNIQUE
VS. OFFENSIVE SETS

More Than Three Yard Split (Force) (Diagram 9-13):

The defensive linebacker should play head up on the offensive end, and then, just prior to the snap of the ball, he should jump back into the force position. Once in the force position, he must set a course for the fullback's original position.

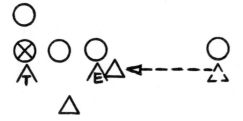

Diagram 9-13

Wing (Regular) (Diagram 9-14):

The linebacker should play regular into the offensive end. He should keep the outside arm loose to deliver a forearm blow whenever the wing back blocks down from the outside. The cornerback may be used in a stunt. The linebacker must listen to the secondary call.

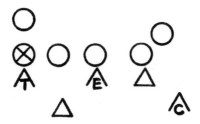

Diagram 9-14

Wing (Stack) (Diagram 9-15):

The defensive end must draw the block of the offensive end by stepping into him and then looping toward the wing back. This opens up a straight path for the linebacker to blitz.

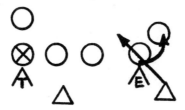

Diagram 9-15

Slot (Hit and Go) (Diagram 9-16):

· If the slot is tight enough, the defensive linebacker should split the offensive end's foot. He should play into the end with the outside foot and deliver a blow with the outside arm. After the blow, he must react to his key. If the end splits out more than five yards, play the slot man just as if he were an offensive end.

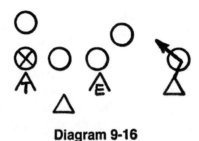

Diagram 9-16

Slot (Charge) (Diagram 9-17):

The defender is coached to charge off the offensive end's outside shoulder, after the defensive end has drawn the offensive tackle's block. The charge must be disguised just prior to the linebacker's move so the slot man will not be able to react and block the linebacker.

Diagram 9-17

Slot (Regular) (Diagram 9-18):

The linebacker is assigned to attack the slot man. The outside is protected by our cornerback, who is moved up tight to the outside. The cornerback's key is the outside man. If the end closes down, the corner man closes down.

Flanker (Regular) (Diagram 9-19):

If the flanker is split three or more yards, the linebacker should use

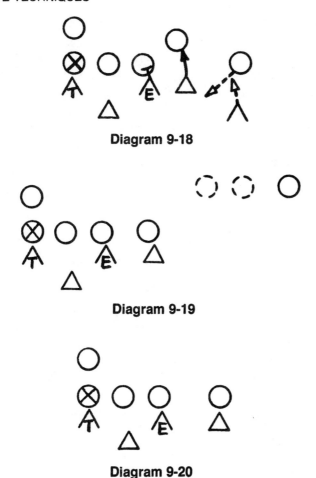

Diagram 9-18

Diagram 9-19

Diagram 9-20

his regular position. He should play his normal technique unless a defensive call changes his assignment. He must penetrate rather than shuffling parallel to the line of scrimmage.

2-3 Yard Split (Regular or Force) (Diagram 9-20):

The defender lines up head up or splitting the end's inside foot. The alignment depends upon the play of the offensive end. He should deliver a blow and react to his key.

SHORTSIDE ADJUSTMENTS

It is apparent today with the modern professional formations, split ends, slots, etc., that the defense must be ready to adjust to a variation of shortside attacks.

The shortside attack presents many defensive problems in that the defensive linebacker has a new alignment. He is continually under offensive pressure in this unique position and must be ready to defend against the shortside tear sweep, the crack back block, the quick "now" pass, the look in pass and many other offensive maneuvers. With these defensive thoughts in mind, the shortside defense is adjusted in several ways. (See Shortside Adjustment, Diagram 9-21).

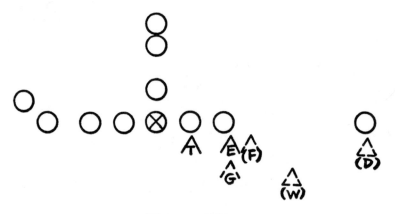

Diagram 9-21

The defender may be placed in a:

"W" position—Off the line of scrimmage equidistant between the defensive tackle and split end.
"F" position—Force position on the line of scrimmage.
"G" position—Go position stacked off the line of scrimmage.
"D" position—Double coverage of a receiver.

We also use defensive calls such as the slide or knock down technique to give our regular defensive lineup a different alignment. The defensive signal caller must be taught when to call our regular defensive calls to and away from the short side. These calls are predicated upon the particular offensive tendencies and personal strength (Diagram 9-21).

PASS CALL

Pass call is usually used by the linebacker who is on the line of scrimmage in a "67" alignment. This alignment and technique could be

used in an over call with two tight ends away from the secondary zone
call. It is also used with a 40 Pro Defense (referred to the normal Pro 43
Defense).

Pass Call Technique (Diagram 9-22):

On all drop back passes, the linebacker ("67") away from the zone
call is coached to key the near back to his side. If the back flares, the

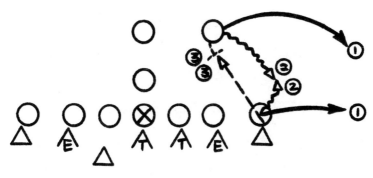

Diagram 9-22

defender plays him man to man if the quarterback drops back to throw a
pocket pass. Whenever the offensive near back breaks directly at the
defender, the linebacker should be taught to knock down the near back
with a forearm blow because the defender does not know if the back is a
potential receiver or a blocker. If the near back sets up to pass block, the
defender is told, "Take Paul to the ball." This means the defender is
coached to run right over the pass protector and take him right to the
passer. The defender should not rush to the blocking back's inside, which
may enable the passer to scramble outside of our pass rush.

"X" Stunt (Diagram 9-23):

The "X" stunt changes up the rush to the split end side. This
defensive stunt gives the "67" man a quick, straight shot into the offensive backfield. His initial target should be the fullback's original position
and his direction is only changed by the backfield's flow. Actually the
"X" stunt features the exchange of defensive assignments between the
end and backer. The end steps into the defensive tackle to help draw the
offensive tackle's block. This gives the charging "67" man a clean shot
into the backfield.

The defensive end must come off his blow and loop to the outside to

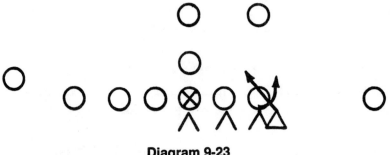

Diagram 9-23

take over the outside contain position, which was vacated by the defensive backer's charging maneuver.

DEFENSIVE TECHNIQUES FOR TACKLE AND END "45"

Tackle Hook Blocks (Diagram 9-24):

The defensive tackle must never let the tackle hook him. This is the most important principle for the defensive "45" technique. The tackle must move on the movement of the offensive tackle's helmet and use his hands to keep the blocker away from getting to his feet and hooking him to the inside. He may have to give ground to avoid being hooked, always fighting through the tackle's head.

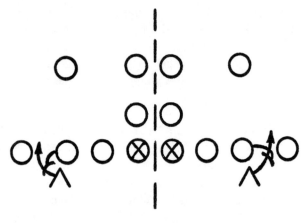

Diagram 9-24

Double Team Block (Diagram 9-25):

Splitting the double team block is one of the methods we teach the defensive tackle. We also coach him to hit the post man and then make an all-out attack on the pressure from the drive blocker. He must whirl out only as a last report, but he must be coached to spin out shallow to the line and stay low. The tackle must never let the double team blockers drive him down the line or backward. He should be ready to drop the outside shoulder and go down to all fours rather than be powered out of his position. If being continually overpowered, he may move back slightly off the line and ask the defensive ''67'' man for more help in hitting the offensive end.

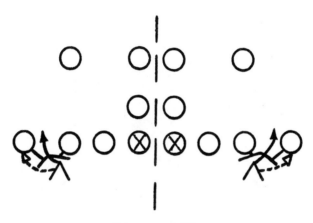

Diagram 9-25

Tackle Blocks to the Inside (Diagram 9-26):

The ''45'' technique should mirror the offensive tackle, and if he releases to the inside, shuffle along with him keeping him off our linebacker. The defender should check for an inside trap or for the end or halfback blocking down.

Tackle Blocks Out (Diagram 9-27):

The defender must deliver a blow on the tackle and fight through his head if the tackle attempts to turn out or use a screen block. The defensive tackle should go directly through the blocker and not circle around him. He should neutralize the blocker with a forearm smash.

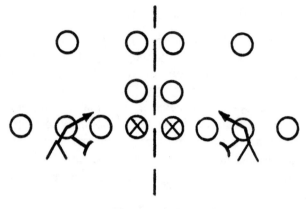

Diagram 9-26

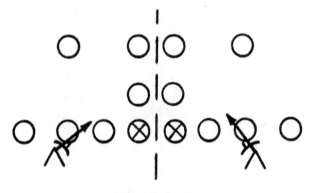

Diagram 9-27

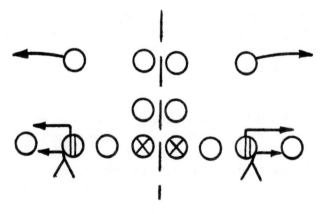

Diagram 9-28

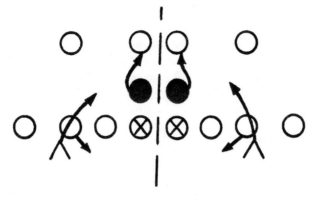

Diagram 9-29

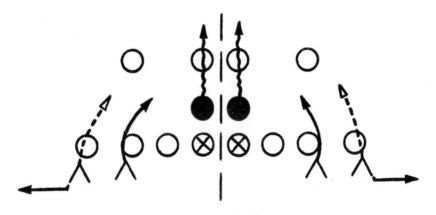

Diagram 9-30

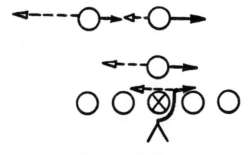

Diagram 9-31

Tackle Pulls Outside (Diagram 9-28):

Once the tackle pulls to the outside, the defensive tackle should make a quick check of the direction of the action and pursue. Next, he should look for the inside threat or possibly the end driving down on him from the outside. If a quick pitch develops, the "45" defender should take a proper flat pursuit course to the ball.

Tackle Releases Across Field (Diagram 9-29):

When the offensive tackle releases to the inside on an across field assignment, the defensive tackle should locate the flow of the ball and trail the play. He should trail the ball carrier, keeping closer to the line of scrimmage than to the ball. Finally, he must look for counter action if the ball goes away from his assigned area.

Tackle Sets Up for Pass (Diagram 9-30):

The defender must rush the passer as soon as the offensive tackle sets up to pass block. He should rush the passer from either inside or outside the blocker, unless the "67" man has pass coverage. If the "67" man has pass coverage, the tackle must rush from the outside executing a contain-rush technique. This is an outside-in rush and should contain any possible outside scrambling by the passer. The defensive tackle should stay within his rushing lane so that the scrambling passer could not pick his way through the rushing defenses.

DEFENSIVE TECHNIQUES FOR THE NOSE TACKLE "0"

Step Around (Diagram 9-31):

This technique should be used by the nose tackle to avoid the center's block and to penetrate into the offensive backfield to destroy the ball carrier.

The coaching point for the step around technique is to take a jab step with the frontside foot in the direction he must go. He should use his hands to push himself away from the center. The defender should be coached to swing the back leg around in a semi-circular action parallel to the other foot, and directly in back of the center's original position. He should shuffle behind the center's position and take a flat pursuit course down the line of scrimmage if action goes away. If action comes the "0" man's way, he should destroy the ball carrier.

Play It Soft (Diagram 9-32):

He must use his arms to keep the center away from his body. The

Diagram 9-32

soft technique enables him to react laterally in any direction; therefore, he should not deliver a hard-nosed forearm blow because the blocker may get into his feet.

Go Technique (Diagram 9-33):

The nose tackle should fire out driving low on all fours straight ahead into the gap, staying low. He must maintain his balance, locate the ball, and make the tackle. If the action goes away, he should take a flat pursuit course and destroy the ball carrier. This technique often causes the opposition to fumble as well as to confuse their blocking assignments.

Diagram 9-33

Off Set Fire Back Into Center (Diagram 9-34):

On the snap of the ball, the "0" defender must fire low into the center. He must hit the center with a forearm blow if he tries to block him, and then react to the ball carrier. His shoulders should be parallel to the line of scrimmage.

Diagram 9-34

DEFENSIVE TECHNIQUES FOR INSIDE LINEBACKERS "223"

Regular Position (Diagram 9-35):

The linebacker's depth should be slightly deeper than the heels of the middle guard. The linebacker should be in a comfortable position so that he can uncoil and deliver a forearm blow into the offensive guard or the first blocker who shows.

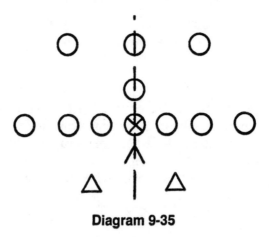

Diagram 9-35

Attack the Guard if They Fire Straight Ahead (Diagram 9-36):

If the linebacker steps into the blocker with his right foot, he should use the same arm to deliver his blow. He must get rid of the blocker as

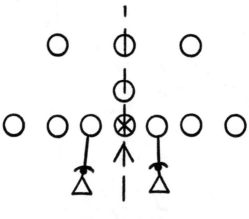

Diagram 9-36

soon as possible by using the other arm to push away the opponent. He must fight through the blocker's head and make sure he never gets hooked. The blocker should step back in a scalloping fashion to make sure he gets rid of the blocker. He should use his hands to push the blocker's head away from his body.

Set Step (Diagram 9-37):

The linebacker must stay low, take a set step, and key. He is coached to cue the halfback and then the backside guard for a trap if the halfback does not come. The fullback may try to torpedo or isolate him. Next, he should check for the tackle blocking down on him in a possible cross blocking or fold blocking situation.

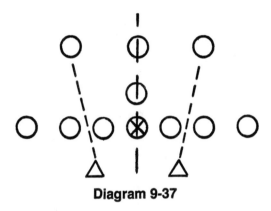

Diagram 9-37

Pass Block Shows (Diagram 9-38):

The linebacker should sprint back into the hook zone quickly and key the quarterback's feet. If any receiver crosses his face, he should knock him down before the ball is in the air. He should not sacrifice lateral movement for depth. He should be under control and in a good football position when the passer throws the ball. If it is deep, he can thud the intended receiver. If it is into the flat, he may lead the interceptor downfield. If the ball is in or near his area, he should go through the receiver for the ball.

If Guards Attempt to Cut Off Linebackers (Diagram 9-39):

He should scallop in the direction of the flow and lose ground slightly if the guard attempts to cut him off. The blocker should fight through the blocker's head and not go inside or he will get cut off. The defender should get rid of the potential blocker and key the ball carrier.

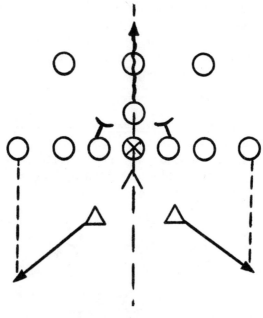

Diagram 9-38

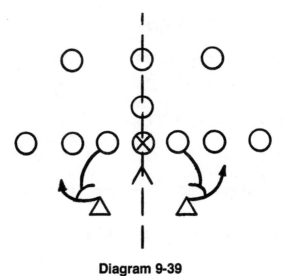

Diagram 9-39

He must keep his shoulders parallel to the line of scrimmage so he can hit through the ball carrier once he turns upfield.

Guard Pulls (Diagram 9-40):

He must scallop laterally to the off-tackle hole checking for the ball carrier to turn upfield if he does not continue scalloping to the outside. He should never overrun the ball. The linebacker should stay slightly behind the ball carrier. Once the guard pulls, he must key the ball carrier and take an intelligent pursuit angle so that he can cut the ball carrier off if he attempts to go wide.

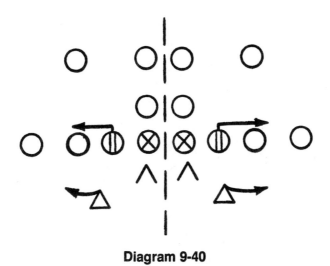

Diagram 9-40

Guard Blocks In and Halfback Tries to Torpedo Linebacker (Diagram 9-41):

The defender should take a set step and be ready to step into and deliver a blow on the halfback. He must fight to get into the running lane, staying low and ready to nail the ball carrier.

Guard Pulls Behind Center (Diagram 9-42):

He must mirror the offensive guard, staying slightly behind the ball carrier's parallel path. The defender must watch for a cutback by the ball carrier. He must scallop to the outside, going over and around bodies, using a good pursuit angle.

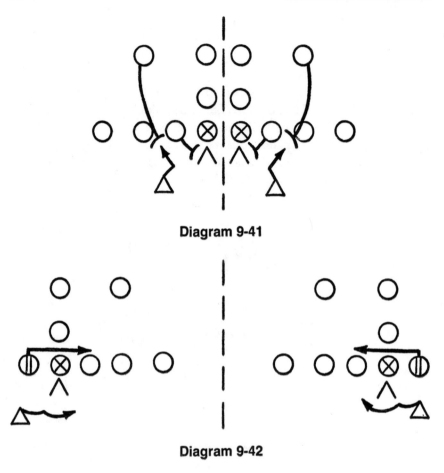

Diagram 9-41

Diagram 9-42

End's Seal Block (Diagram 9-43):

He should be ready for the end to crack back as the ball carrier begins his sweep outside. He must never go inside the end, as he may not cut off the ball carrier.

Guard Blocks Inside, Tackle Blocks Inside (Diagram 9-44):

The defender must take a set step and pick out the ball carrier. He must be ready to be blocked from the outside, by the tackle or end. The linebacker must be aware of either the trap or the back's torpedo or isolation block.

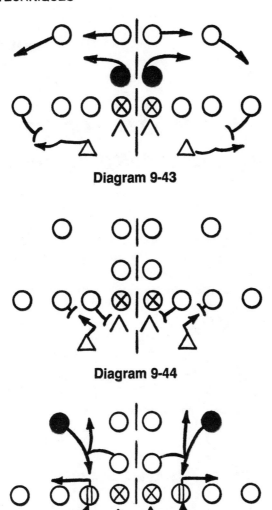

Diagram 9-43

Diagram 9-44

Diagram 9-45

False Key with Ball Carrier Running Inside (Diagram 9-45):

The defender is taught to key the frontside back through the guard. He should begin to scallop to the outside, then change his direction. He must keep his shoulders parallel to the line of scrimmage in order to hit the ball carrier head on.

Chapter 10

How to Stunt from the
Forty Over and Under Defenses

If Forty Under Defense is called, the defensive signal caller simply calls "41 Under," and the defensive stunt is the same as the "41" or Split 41 Defenses. The defensive left tackle still stunts into the "1" gap, the weakside defensive end loops outside, and these two moves enable the weakside linebacker to fire through the "3" gap (Diagram 10-1).

A "42 Under Call' (Diagram 10-2) assigns the defensive left tackle to loop through the "1" gap. This is the defensive tackle's normal loop off a "2" call, only from the "40" and Split 40 Defense the defensive left tackle was head up on the strongside guard or outside shoulder of the strongside guard. The linebacker ("223") blitzes into the "3" gap.

The "43" call is changed to a 43 Switch call which sends the defensive end through the "5" gap and the "3" linebacker to the outside (Diagram 10-3).

FORTY UNDER—CRASH LUCKY (Diagram 10-4)

When Crash Lucky is called and the ball comes to the defender's left, the left end uses his crash technique. The left end lines up on the outside shoulder of the offensive right tackle ("45" alignment) and crashes over the offensive right guard's outside shoulder. The linebacker to the same side ("223" technique) lines up similar to an Oklahoma linebacker, scrapes off and replaces the left end. If the quarterback or action goes away from the scrape off linebacker's side (dotted line), the "45" defender still crashes, but the linebacker disregards his scrape off technique and pursues the ball carrier. It is most important that the linebacker scrapes off as close as possible to the "45" defensive area. If he overruns this area he will open up the funnel for the ball carrier, which could result in a long gainer.

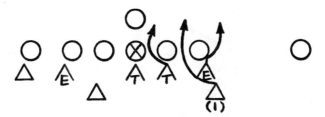

41 UNDER

Diagram 10-1

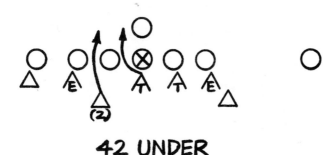

42 UNDER

Diagram 10-2

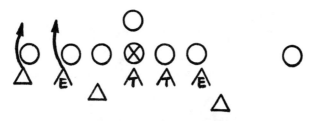

43 SWITCH UNDER

Diagram 10-3

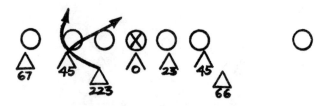

40 UNDER CRASH LUCKY

Diagram 10-4

The 40 Under Crash Lucky alignment gives us an Oklahoma or 50 Defensive look from the center to the defensive left. This Oklahoma look is the result of moving the left tackle from his customary "2" position to a nose up "0" or middle guard-like alignment.

In our defensive playbook, we simply list our defensive assignments in this manner:

Crash Lucky:

LLB—Regular "67"
LB—Crash
MLB—Scrape Off
LT—Regular "0"
RLB—Regular "66"
RT—Regular "23"
RE—Regular "45"

FORTY UNDER—CRASH RINGO (Diagram 10-5)

Crash Ringo is much the same as Crash Lucky in the previous diagram. Since Crash Ringo is called versus a split end formation, the 40

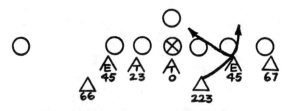

40 UNDER CRASH RINGO

Diagram 10-5

Under alignment specifies that the right tackle, originally lined up in his regular "2" (40 alignment), moves under or toward the weak or split end side. This, of course, places the middle linebacker in a "223" or Oklahoma-like defensive position, shading the offensive left guard's outside shoulder.

This call is used to confuse the offensive blocking and is also used as a penetrating defense. This defense is strong against the off-tackle plays and against sprint out passes. The defensive coaching staff emphasizes the following coaching points:

1. The linebacker ("223") must scallop quickly toward action as soon as he determines flow has gone away.
2. If flow comes toward the linebacker, he should continue his stunt.
3. The linebacker has the option of chasing behind a pulling guard occasionally, if a stunt has not been called to his side.
4. The linebacker must be alert for all counter plays.
5. On all normal non-stunting defenses, the linebackers should call "Lucky" or "Ringo," but these would be false calls and meaningless to all of the defenders.
6. On hard-nose over or under calls, all defenders should crowd the ball and play tougher.
7. The hard-nose calls are strong against trapping and pulling offensive teams.
8. If a drop back pass shows, the stunting linebacker should continue through with his stunt.
9. The red dogging linebacker must always make it to his predesignated alignment point. He must never go off route for a fake or be cut off by an opponent's block.

Crash Ringo Defensive Assignments:

LE—Regular "45"
LT—Regular "23"
LLB—Regular "66"
RT—Regular "0"
MLB—Scrape Off
RE—Crash
RLB—Regular "67"

FORTY OVER—SQUEEZE LUCKY (Diagram 10-6)

The Squeeze Lucky is a stronger defensive stunt against the off-

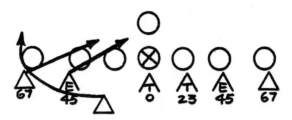

40 OVER SQUEEZE LUCKY

Diagram 10-6

tackle maneuver than the Crash stunt. The Squeeze Lucky crashes both the left linebacker and left end over the inside shoulders of the offensive man to their inside, respectively. The inside linebacker is assigned to scrape off to the defensive "67" position. If action goes away, the "223" linebacker should scallop and pursue the action. The linebacker may occasionally take the option and shoot behind the pulling guard, if action goes away, and take a flat course to head off the ball carrier.

The left tackle moves over to a nose up position on the center and plays his assignment similarly to an Oklahoma middle guard. The other three defenders, to the strong side, split the outside leg of the offensive left guard, tackle, and end.

The defensive play book lists the 40 Over Squeeze Lucky stunts as follows:

LLB—Pinch
LE—Crash
MLB—Scrape Off
LT—Regular "0"
RLB—Regular "67"
RT—Regular "23"
RE—Regular "45

FORTY UNDER—SQUEEZE RINGO (Diagram 10-7)

The Squeeze stunt is not only a fine defensive stunt against the off-tackle play, but it is also a good call against the sweep and the sprint out pass. This stunt penetrates against both of these offensive plays and is a difficult stunt against man to man offensive blocking teams. Even when the play goes away from the Squeeze stunt, the backside defensive blitz has proven most successful in pressuring the ball carrier or the passer from the back or blind side.

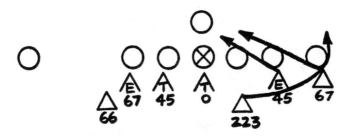

40 OVER SQUEEZE RINGO

Diagram 10-7

Coaching points pertaining to this stunt include:

1. The nose tackle must be able to protect both sides of the center when this stunt is called. At times, we move the nose man a yard to a yard and one-half back from his original alignment.
2. Whenever a defender is called to pinch, he should take more of a head up alignment on the offensive man rather than shading the defender's outside body.
3. A safety blitz is also a good call to the opposite side of the line versus two tight ends. This allows our defense an all-out rush through all of the offensive gaps.
4. The scrape off linebacker must get to the ''67'' position as soon as possible.
5. The scrape off linebacker must not overrun his predetermined area by bowing too wide outside the ''67'' position.
6. The squeezing defenders are taught to squeeze as quickly as possible, aiming directly for their defensive spots and tackle the ball carrier high and quickly, to force a fumble.

The defender's Squeeze Ringo assignments are:

LE—Regular ''45''
LT—Regular ''23''
LLB—Regular ''66''
RT—Regular ''0''
MLB—Scrape Off
RE—Crash
RLB—Squeeze

FORTY OVER—SQUEEZE RINGO (Diagram 10-8)

The Squeeze stunt also is called and executed to the short or split side of the offensive formation. The defensive right end moves into the "67" force position and fires off the outside shoulder of the offensive

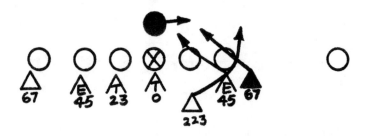

Diagram 10-8

shortside tackle. The defensive right tackle angles to the outside shoulder of the offensive shortside guard, and the "223" linebacker scrapes off to the original position of the defensive end and squares his shoulders off, playing a "45" technique once he arrives at his predetermined position. All of the other defenders play their normal Forty Over assignments.

FORTY OVER—RINGO LOOP (Diagram 10-9)

Using the same defensive alignment call against two tight ends, the Loop Ringo Call loops the right linebacker, end, and the nose tackle all to the right gaps. The "223" linebacker plays his normal read, keying the offensive guard. The left defensive tackle uses a half loop and fires into the head of the offensive guard from his "23" position.

FORTY OVER—RINGO ZOOM (Diagram 10-10)

This defensive stunt calls for the "223" linebacker to blitz straight through the "1" gap. This area is opened up by the nose tackle looping

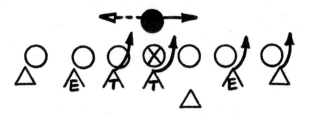

40 OVER RINGO LOOP

Diagram 10-9

40 OVER RINGO ZOOM

Diagram 10-10

into the opposite "1" gap, drawing the center's block. The defensive right end lines up in a "4" alignment and then loops into the "3" gap, which may draw the block of the offensive left guard. This allows the linebacker to shoot through the "1" gap unobstructed.

There are only a handfull of stunts that can be used from the Forty Over or Under calls. The continual shifting from the Forty or Split Forty to the Forty Over and Under calls, plus the stunts and blitzes from this odd defensive look, helps to keep the offensive quarterback guessing. This defense has proven to be a valuable defensive change-up.

FORTY OVER AND UNDER DRILLS

The Forty Over and Under Drills are the same drills we use in our Forty and Split Forty Defenses.

Chapter 11

Forty Stack Defense

(Diagram 11-1)—The Forty Stack Defense places both the defensive tackles in the "1" and "3" gaps and stacks a linebacker behind both of these linemen. These gap defenders add another look to the offensive attack. The tackles' "Go" techniques, backed up by the linebackers' reading and blitzing assignments, make this Forty Look a difficult defense to block. Normal offensive word and number blocking rules have to be adjusted whenever the offensive attack attempts to run inside of the gap-stacked defenders.

The Forty Stack Defense is also an easy front to shift from to another Forty defensive call. The Forty Stack alignment is also an excellent defense to adjust to offensive backfield shifts just prior to the snap of the ball. It is also a strong basic defense to direct a Veer call to an anticipated offensive point of attack. We use the gap stacks to minimize the maximum offensive line splits used by many of our opponents.

FORTY STACK LUCKY (Diagram 11-2)

Basically, we direct the "1" gap stack to the side of the tight end. The left linebacker lines up in a "67" alignment which moves the defensive end into a "45" alignment, which he uses in our Forty Pro, Over-Under, Goal Line, etc., calls. The normal forty tackle moves from a head up alignment into a "1" gap alignment, and the middle linebacker moves over from his "00" alignment to a stacked "11" position. Our right tackle moves from his "2" alignment into the "3" gap area, and the right linebacker stacks behind him. The right defensive end lines up in a "45" alignment to the split side.

If the offensive attack features two tight ends, we will place the "1" gap stack to the wide side of the field or to the side of the opponent's most powerful runners or strongest blockers. This defensive strategy will be predicated upon by our scouting reports and opponent's film breakdowns.

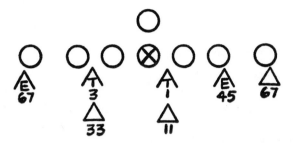

FORTY STACK RINGO

Diagram 11-1

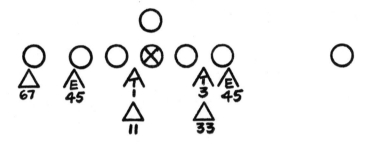

FORTY STACK LUCKY

Diagram 11-2

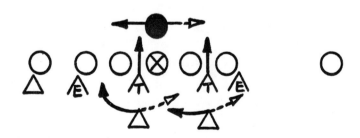

FORTY STACK LUCKY

Diagram 11-3

FORTY STACK STUNTS

Forty Stack Lucky (Diagram 11-3):

The stack read game again calls for both of the linemen in their stacks to fire across on all fours using their "Go" techniques. We usually put our middle linebacker to the offensive strength (in this case, toward the tight end's side). We want our gapped linemen to penetrate, and our linebackers are coached to read their keys and scallop toward the flow. The linebackers must always be concerned about counter plays. This stacked alignment gives the offensive blockers a different blocking look, and it is a good defense to stunt from or play normal defense.

> LLB—Regular "67"
> LE—Regular "45"
> MLB—Read "11"
> LT—"Go" "11"
> RLB—Read "33"
> RT—"Go" "3"
> RE—"45"

Forty Stack Ringo (Diagram 11-4):

Same as the above Stack Lucky defense, only the call is "Ringo."

> LE—"45"
> LT—"Go" "3"
> LLB—Read "33"
> RT—"Go" "1"
> MLB—Read "11"
> RE—Regular "45"
> RLB—Regular "67"

FORTY STACK BLITZ STUNTS

Forty Stack Blitz Lucky (Diagram 11-5):

Both of our stacked linebackers key the quarterback and blitz into the nearest gap to the direction of the quarterback. The left end and tackle play their regular Forty Stack techniques and our right end plays a "67" technique. The defensive left and right tackles fire out into their assigned gaps on all fours, penetrating into the offensive backfield.

This defense develops into a gap defense to the side of the quarterback's course with defenders in every gap toward the point of

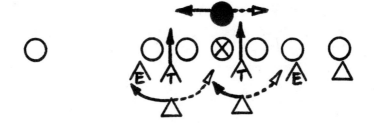

FORTY STACK RINGO

Diagram 11-4

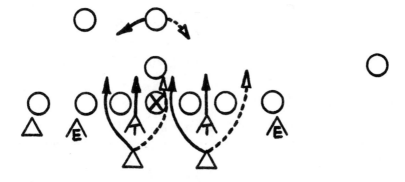

FORTY STACK BLITZ LUCKY

Diagram 11-5

attack. We want our left tackle to stack away from the split end. The stack blitz is most effective against the inside running attack and the sprint out action. We always have our linebackers to the side of the action because they key the quarterback's course.

 LLB—Regular "67"
 LE—Regular "45"
 MLB—Blitz "11"
 LT—"Go" "1"
 RLB—Blitz "33"
 RT—"Go" "3"
 RE—Regular "67"

Forty Stack Blitz Ringo (Diagram 11-6):

Same as the above Stack Blitz, only we call it to the right.

LE—Regular "67"
LT—"Go" "3"
LLB—Blitz "33"
RT—"Go" "1"
MLB—Blitz "11"
RE—Regular "45"
RLB—Regular "67"

Forty Stack Ringo Veer (Diagram 11-7):

The defensive right tackle lines up in the "1" gap. The defensive tackle is coached to fire directly through the center's head. As soon as the defender reaches this point, he is taught to level off, squaring his shoulders to the line of scrimmage. (If the offensive guard takes a maximum split, the defender is taught to fire straight through the "1" gap, as deep as the offensive blocker's original heel alignment. Once the defensive tackle reaches this depth, he is taught to take a correct pursuit course to the ball.)

The reason the defensive right tackle is taught to drive directly into the center's head is to make sure the center is unable to block the right linebacker.

The defensive left tackle lines up in the "3" gap and is coached to drive through the head of the offensive right guard. As soon as the defender executes a veer charge, he is taught to square off to the line of scrimmage. This defender is coached to never get trapped. If the defender feels a potential trap is aimed his way, he is taught to get lower than the trap and meet the blocker with a blow with his inside arm, while stepping with his inside leg and keeping both shoulders parallel to the line of scrimmage. We do not want the defender to turn the entire body to attack the potential trapper, because he will not have his back foot anchored to meet the force of the trapper's block. Keeping the defender's shoulders parallel to the line of scrimmage also enables the blocker to pursue in any direction, if the ball carrier decides to run to daylight at the last moment. The defensive left tackle's parallel stance also helps the blocker meet the block from his left side, if the offense uses a fake trap block action to draw the defensive tackle toward the center.

The right end lines head up on the offensive tackle in a "4" technique and veers inside, tight over the original position of the guard's outside shoulder. If the offensive tackle attempts a cut-off block, the defensive

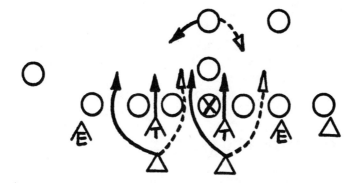

FORTY STACK BLITZ RINGO

Diagram 11-6

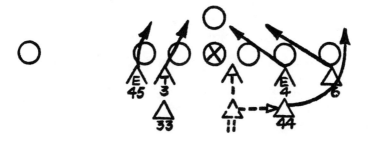

STACK RINGO VEER

Diagram 11-7

end is coached to drive straight through the offensive blocker's neck.

The right linebacker lines up in a "6" alignment and then slants down to the original position of the offensive tackle's shoulder.

The right inside linebacker moves over from his stacked position behind the defensive right tackle ("11" technique) and lines up stacked behind the defensive end's position ("44" alignment). Just as the center snaps the ball, the right inside linebacker is coached to scrape off to a tight position where the offensive end originally lined up. The linebacker reaches his "67" alignment on the run, and is now coached to read the flow just like a defender playing the "67" assignment. He must keep his shoulders parallel to the line of scrimmage.

The defensive left end plays his regular "45" position, and keys the offensive tackle until he picks up (reads) the flow of the offensive backs and the offensive blocking pattern.

The defensive left inside linebacker stacks behind the offensive left tackle in his "33" position and keys the quarterback.

FORTY STACKED LINEBACKER'S REACTION

"33" Alignment/Technique (Left Inside Linebacker) (Diagram 11-8):

1. Play Action Pass: If committed—Attack the passer.
2. Play Action Pass: If not committed—Sprint to split side hook zone. If offensive halfback is running a divide pass course, collision the potential receiver; then check hook zone.
3. Pocket Pass: Protect hook zone to your side.
4. Sprint Out Pass: Protect hook zone to your side.

"11" Alignment/Technique (Right Inside Linebacker) (Diagram 11-8):

1. Play Action Pass *Away*: Check run, then drop back deep middle. If split side linebacker is committed to the possible run, check frontside hook area.
2. Pocket Pass: Drop back to hook zone to your side.
3. Sprint Out Pass *Away*: Check backside hook; no one there, then drop back to deep middle area.

Forty Stack Ringo Load (Diagram 11-9):

The Stack Load Defense is a stunt used to get four defenders to the strong side quickly. This stunt is usually used against a team who likes to sprint out, sweep, or run power plays off tackle. The right inside linebacker lines up in his regular "11" alignment and then shuffles over stacked behind the defensive right end in a "445" alignment. Just as the ball is snapped, the right inside linebacker is coached to shoot into the "3" gap and make something happen. The blitzing backer must be under control so that he can locate the ball and then take the proper angle to get to the ball as quickly as possible.

The "21" defender must get a piece of the offensive guard's inside

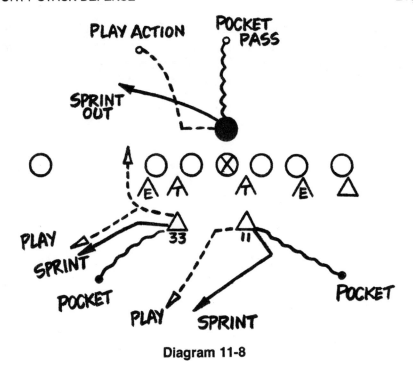

Diagram 11-8

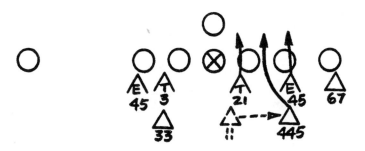

STACK RINGO LOAD

Diagram 11-9

shoulder so that the guard will block him. The "45" defensive end must drive through the offensive left tackle's outside shoulder so that the tackle will block the defensive end. This will enable the "445" linebacker to fire through unmolested into the opponent's backfield.

Index